Sweeter
THAN
Honey

A BIBLE STUDY ON ENJOYING
GOD IN HIS WORD

BY MAGGIE COMBS
AND GRETCHEN SAFFLES

Sweeter than Honey: A Bible Study on Enjoying God in His Word

All Scripture quotations are from *The Holy Bible*, English Standard Version® (ESV®), copyright © 2001 by Crossway, a publishing ministry of Good News Publishers. Used by permission. All rights reserved. ESV® Text Edition: 2016.

Designed in the U.S.A.

Published in association with the literary agency of Wolgemuth & Wilson.

Written by Maggie Combs and Gretchen Saffles. Design by Kercia Mueller. Content edit by Lauren Weir. Copy edit by Abbey Wysocki. Original artwork by Heather Powers. Hand lettering by Naomi Dable of Naomi Paper Co. Author photographs by Anna Grace Fulmer.

For information about special discounts for bulk purchases, please contact Tyndale House Publishers at csresponse@tyndale.com or call 1-855-277-9400.

tyndale.com

ISBN 979-8-4005-0194-4

Printed in China

30	29	28	27	26	25	24
7	6	5	4	3	2	1

Table of Contents

About the Authors...05

Before You Begin Your Study...06

Introductory Session Viewer Guide..07

Week One | Study the Word..08

Session One Viewer Guide..27

Week Two | The Unchanging Word..28

Session Two Viewer Guide...47

Week Three | The Good News of the Word....................................48

Session Three Viewer Guide..69

Week Four | Transformed by the Word..70

Session Four Viewer Guide..87

Week Five | The Word in Every Season...88

Session Five Viewer Guide..107

Week Six | The Word in Everyday Life...108

Session Six Viewer Guide...129

Build Your Bible Study Library..130

Main Idea Examples...131

About the Authors

MAGGIE COMBS is the author of several Bible studies, *Motherhood Without All the Rules*, and *Unsupermommy*. Maggie is passionate about encouraging women to grow in holiness as they grow in relationship with God. She loves playing games with her husband and three boys, herding fainting goats on their family farm, and reading cozy mysteries. It is her joy to serve in her local church through teaching women and children about the Bible and discipling young women.

GRETCHEN SAFFLES is the founder of Well-Watered Women and the author of *Word before World: 100 Devotions to Put Jesus First, The Well-Watered Woman*, and several Bible studies. She is passionate about encouraging and equipping women to drink deeply from the well of God's Word and longs to see women grasp the fullness of the gospel in everyday life. Gretchen loves going on adventures with her husband and three kids, traveling to new places, baking chocolate chip cookies, reading good books, and teaching women to know and love Jesus.

Before You Begin Your Study

At Well-Watered Women, we're passionate about helping women grow their love for God and his Word through engaging and theologically-rich Bible study. You can complete this Bible study on your own, but we highly recommend gathering in fellowship with at least one other woman in your local area to dig into God's Word together. Each day begins with instruction on Bible study principles and methods, then includes Bible study practice using three principles: gather knowledge, digest the big ideas, and grow in godliness. Whether you've been studying God's Word for years or are just learning the basics, this study will equip you to use these principles as you study God's Word every day in every season.

This study also includes:

- Seven teaching sessions with Gretchen and Maggie available for purchase at TyndaleChristianResources.com
- A free leader guide available for download at TyndaleChristianResources.com
- Questions that will be clearest using the English Standard Version (ESV) translation of the Bible
- A free printable of all the Bible study questions found throughout the study available for download at wellwateredwomen.com/sweeterthanhoney

So sink into your couch or pull out a chair at your kitchen table and get ready to feast on the goodness of God's Word.

Introductory Session Viewer Guide

Teaching sessions available for purchase at TyndaleChristianResources.com

_____

_____

_____

_____

_____

_____

_____

_____

_____

_____

_____

_____

_____

_____

_____

_____

_____

QUESTIONS FOR DISCUSSION OR REFLECTION

What obstacles to Bible study do you face?

How do you hope to grow through this Bible study?

Study the Word

The advances of technology have built a nearly instantaneous life for many people in the world. From two-hour delivery of toilet paper to the dopamine hit of likes on a social media post, our desires are being trained to expect immediate attention. Yet these quick fixes leave an underlying hunger—while our material desires are momentarily satiated, our souls remain spiritually malnourished.

All over nature, we see that fruitfulness requires time, careful cultivation, and the work of a sovereign God. On the pages of Scripture, it's evident that God is not quick to alleviate people's painful circumstances. Instead, God uses suffering to transform us, cultivating holiness through his careful and kind tending. After Adam and Eve sinned in the garden of Eden, God could have immediately sent Jesus Christ, but he didn't. God took his time, drawing a people near to him, teaching them his faithfulness through suffering and rescuing and redeeming them over and over until, at the exact right time, Jesus came into the world. He lived, suffered, died, and rose again to defeat sin and death for all who would call upon his name and follow him.

So when we open our Bibles, we shouldn't expect the instant encouragement of an Instagram post or the quick fix of googled answers for all our problems. The Bible isn't an instruction manual or a self-help encyclopedia. It's the very Word of God written to his people that they may know him intimately, trust in his faithfulness, and experience his redemption. So come to your Bible not to check reading it off your list, to achieve good Christian status, or even to fix your problems with a scan of the page and a quickly chosen verse. Come to your Bible to know your God deeply and experience the slow process of becoming more like your Savior. May the Holy Spirit use Scripture to grow your love for him.

Day One | Sweeter than Honey

Every few months, I decide I'm going to become a tea drinker. I pull out all my tea supplies from the back of the cupboard: loose leaf tea canisters, sieve, teacup, and most importantly, my prized local honey. The highlight of drinking tea, in my opinion, is the honey.

On a trip to Carmel Valley Ranch in California, my husband and I saw firsthand the intricate process of how honey is made. Dressed in white beekeeping suits complete with veiled hoods, we followed our instructor to a myriad of bustling beehive boxes where we witnessed the majestic wonder of the worker bees transforming nectar into honey.

Did you know that an average worker bee will only produce 1/12 of a teaspoon of honey in its short lifetime? In order for honey bees to make just one pound of honey, they must gather nectar from about two million flowers. And another mind-boggling fact: when properly preserved, honey never expires. The longest preserved pure honey is estimated to be about 5,500 years old. [1]

In Psalm 119, the psalmist likens the treasure of God's Word to the delectable taste of honey: "How sweet are your words to my taste, sweeter than honey to my mouth!" (v. 103). Honey delights our taste buds, but God's Word delights our souls. The more you taste the goodness of God in his life-giving Word, the more you'll crave it over the temporary pleasures of this world.

God faithfully preserves every promise in his Word. May we discover, like the psalmist, that his words are sweeter than honey—a gift to us from our Creator to enjoy as we delight in him.

Gretchen Saffles

My husband has wanted to keep bees for years, but I've always resisted. We live on a small hobby farm and keep goats and cows and even a donkey, so bees aren't that far-fetched. But bees produce honey, and honey has to be collected and shared or sold, and that has always felt like just too much to deal with. The idea reminds me of when a friend shared her "easy" recipe for homemade almond milk with me—it only included eleven steps, one of which was pouring pulverized almonds through a cheesecloth and squeezing all the juice (or milk?) out. So easy, right? I'm not the kind of person who enjoys the process. Why spend all the effort caring for bees when honey—or almond milk—is so easy to buy? Just give me the results.

I can bring that same kind of attitude to God's Word. I want to essentially purchase the sweet honey of knowing God in his Word by checking off the tasks of a Bible reading plan instead of entering into the process. Bible study can feel laborious at times, and I want the fruit without the effort. It seems like some women are so good at following an eleven-step daily study routine. To them, it's as easy as making their own almond milk or keeping bees. These women seem to have discovered some secret, when they've just learned to love the process instead of obsessing over results.

I recently reconnected with an old friend who values process over results. She moved back to our home state of Minnesota, sacrificing the lovely little piece of land she lived on in Washington and losing her favorite hobby— beekeeping. When I told her about my husband's dream of keeping bees, she immediately offered to teach us everything we would need to know. Sometimes, when the process feels overwhelming or exhausting or too complicated, we really just need a friend to come alongside us and say, "Let me show you how." That's the goal of this study.

If you feel ill-equipped or overwhelmed or like you just aren't a process kind of person, we hope to simplify and demystify studying God's Word by sharing three principles to guide your study process. We pray that this study helps you grow to love studying your Bible as it grows your love for God himself. Because unlike honey or almond milk, you can't buy an intimate relationship with the God of the universe at a grocery store. It begins with salvation through Jesus Christ and matures through knowing and enjoying God in his Word.

Maggie Combs

SWEETER THAN HONEY HEART CHECK

What hobbies, activities, or social events do you enjoy?

How are these things like or unlike Bible study?

What keeps you from opening God's Word? Consider the following categories and try to list one to three obstacles in each one.

Physical environment

Physical limitations

Mental hurdles

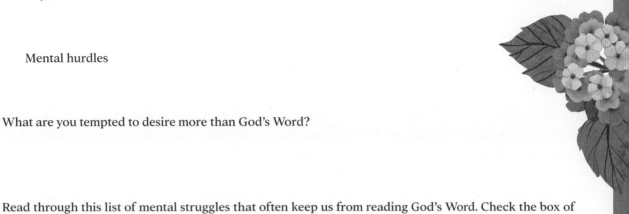

What are you tempted to desire more than God's Word?

Read through this list of mental struggles that often keep us from reading God's Word. Check the box of any that you tell yourself.

- ☐ I'm not academic enough to study the Bible.
- ☐ I don't have time to study the Bible.
- ☐ The Old Testament is too confusing to understand.
- ☐ I know I *should* study my Bible, but I just don't feel like it.
- ☐ I don't need to study my Bible because I listen to so many Christian podcasts, sermons, or Bible teachers or read so many Christian books, emails, or social media posts.
- ☐ The Bible is so old and out of touch; it can't help me with the struggles of my daily life.
- ☐ I'm afraid of how I might feel convicted or sinful if I study the Bible.
- ☐ I'll never love the Bible the way other women do.
- ☐ There's only one right way to study my Bible, so I must be doing it wrong.
- ☐ I must come away from my Bible study encouraged or with a specific nugget of truth for my day.
- ☐ Good Christians don't struggle to read their Bible.

What difference do you hope completing *Sweeter than Honey* will make in your current experience with or attitude toward Bible study?

Review your answers to today's heart check and write a prayer asking the Holy Spirit to work in your heart and mind to transform your Bible study experience.

Day Two | Gather

It's easy to swing between two extremes when we read our Bibles—simply opening to any page and expecting God to speak directly to our lives without making an effort to understand the meaning of the passage, or looking to a rigorous process of Bible study to make sure we do it just right. If you tend to open your Bible just to search for the nearest answer to a problem in your life, you might sense that you're missing something, some bigger picture. If you've tried and failed to follow an intense and intricate Bible study process or never even had the energy to start, we hope to equip you with knowledge and confidence.

This study will teach you how to dig into God's Word, understand it, and apply it by learning three key principles of Bible study: **gather knowledge**, **digest the big ideas**, and **grow in godliness**. These principles will help you faithfully interpret Scripture while adapting the exact process to your personality, your season of life, the book of the Bible you're studying, and even your study goals. The first week of study presents an overview of these three principles. In each following week, you'll dig deeper into each one, practicing them all as you go.

The first principle of Bible study is to gather knowledge. Like a forager bee gathering nectar from flowers to produce honey, we must diligently search God's Word to gather the knowledge that will be digested into understanding. This is more than speed reading the pages of your Bible. This is slowing down, seeking to understand, and gathering only what already exists. In the same way that you might start a new relationship by asking intentional questions about a person's past, preferences, and personality, gathering knowledge through careful attention to God's Word deepens your relationship with him.

Gathering knowledge looks like thoughtfully reading the text and asking yourself, *What does this passage say?* It's easy to assume you know what the Bible says based on previous readings, sermons or podcasts you've listened to, or what that wise woman said on social media, but this principle asks you to leave behind what you think these verses mean and only gather what is actually presented.

Gathering knowledge is a commitment to considering the context of the passage. How would the original hearers of the passage have understood it as they listened to it, recited it, and sung it in their own context? How have generations of believers understood it since then based on the story of Scripture, the historical context, and the genre and literary style? Don't worry if you don't know what any of those terms mean—you'll spend the next two weeks learning and practicing how to gather that knowledge. While it's tempting to speed through this to get to big ideas and applications, gathering knowledge about the text is actually the most time-consuming portion of studying God's Word. Like a bee's relentless pursuit of nectar, studying the Bible diligently takes discipline, but over time, it produces a delight that's sweeter than honey.

Each day, you'll practice the three principles of Bible study: gather, digest, and grow. At the beginning, we'll give you helpful questions to complete each principle, but as you practice and get more comfortable, we'll slowly take off the training wheels so that by the end of this study, you're confident in using these three principles on your own.

 Pray for humility and insight before you study God's Word.

GATHER KNOWLEDGE

Read Deuteronomy 6:1–15 to grasp the larger context of today's passage. Who are the original hearers of this passage (v. 3)?

Look back at Deuteronomy 5:1. Who is speaking in this passage?

Return to Deuteronomy 6 and read verses 5–9 again. What commandment is given in verse 5?

How are the Israelites instructed to interact with the commandments of God in verses 6–9? Summarize the shall statements below.

Verse 6

Verse 7

Verse 8

Verse 9

How much of a person's day is encompassed by the actions in verse 7 (sitting, walking, lying down, rising)?

How are the actions described in the shall statements of verses 6–9 necessary for keeping the command to love God with all your heart, soul, and might?

DIGEST THE BIG IDEAS

You'll learn more about this principle in tomorrow's study, but expect these questions to help you dig deeper into the text, engaging your heart, soul, and might in your study of God's Word.

What do you think is Moses' purpose for speaking the shall statements in verses 6–9 to the Israelites?

Look at verses 10–15. What does Moses warn the people against in verse 12?

Look back at verses 1–3. Why should the Israelites work so hard to understand and remember God's commands?

What is the main idea of verses 4–9? (Note: See page 131 for an example response. Examples are provided until you complete Week Four Day Two on how to digest the main idea of a passage. Don't worry if your main idea is different from the one we identified. The purpose of this study is to help you learn to discern God's Word for yourself.)

The final question you will engage with regularly in this section will help you step back and see the bigger picture of what God is revealing about his character, the work of his Son, and his plan of redemption. Consider this question an opportunity for you to know and love God more.

What did you learn about God, Jesus Christ, or the gospel from today's study?

GROW IN GODLINESS

How might the main idea of Deuteronomy 6:4–9 apply to your circumstances?

Circle the way you will respond to God's Word today.

Today I will...   believe   act   repent   worship   pray

Use this space for your response or to plan how you will respond throughout your day.

Write the verse, attribute of God, or gospel truth you will meditate on today.

Day Three | Digest

Just as nectar doesn't immediately transform into honey when gathered by bees, the knowledge we gather in Bible study isn't immediately easy to comprehend or apply. Digestion is a process that will regularly stretch beyond the allotted thirty minutes we usually set aside for Bible study. This doesn't mean you need to spend all day studying your Bible. It means that, like the command to the Israelites that you looked at yesterday, you continue to digest what you learned as you studied your Bible as you go about your day—walking, eating meals, going to work, washing dishes, talking with family and friends, laying down at night—remembering it long after you close your Bible.

Forager bees are responsible for gathering nectar, flitting from flower to flower, searching for sweet juice to consume and store in their honey stomachs. A forager bee might have to drink from more than a thousand flowers to fill its honey stomach—that's a lot of gathering! Once the nectar enters the honey stomach, digestive enzymes start to break it down, beginning the honey-making process. Back at the hive, the forager bee passes its load off to another worker bee, who passes it off to another, and then another. The best description I've heard for this process is a game of "regurgitation telephone."[2] After many rounds of digestion and regurgitation, the nectar is placed in a comb and the bees beat their wings over it until it's distilled down into honey.

Like the forager bee, our process of gathering is often a slow and painstaking process of returning to God's Word over and over again. Some days, this might be the only principle you're able to complete. Later in this study, we'll share different methods for incorporating these principles in different seasons within the limitations that God has given you. For now, know that diligently returning to God's Word is necessary to build delight in God's Word. But once we've gathered, it's time to digest what we've found, rolling it around in our minds and hearts, distilling all that knowledge down into the big ideas of the passage.

The fancy theologian word for this process is *hermeneutics*. Even if you don't realize it, you're always interpreting the meaning of what you're reading. Think of a word as simple as *boot*. Depending on your circumstances and background, you might imagine a rain or snow boot, a pair of booties, a cowboy boot, a steel-toed work boot, or, if you're from across the pond, the storage section of a car. You interpret the meaning of *boot* based on the knowledge you've gathered.

In *How to Read the Bible for All Its Worth*, professors Gordon D. Fee and Douglas Stuart explain, "The aim of good interpretation is simple: to get at the 'plain meaning of the text.' And the most important ingredient one brings to

this task is enlightened common sense."[3] Faithful gathering enables you to digest the big ideas and interpret the meaning of a passage through the power of the Holy Spirit.

So the second principle of Bible study is to digest the big ideas. When you digest the big ideas, you'll be looking for the plain meaning of that portion of Scripture. You're moving from the gathering stage where you asked, *What does it say?* to the deeper question, *What does it mean?* Remember: a biblical text can't mean what it never meant, so you need to digest the big ideas of the passage of Scripture you're studying before moving on to applying it to your life.[4]

When we dig deeper into this principle in Week Four, we'll show you how to identify the main idea, confirm your understanding against other passages in Scripture, and determine what the passage displays about God's character, the story of Jesus Christ across all of Scripture, and the gospel. As you grow in your ability to digest the big ideas, the Bible's themes will begin to emerge. Then you'll see how all the parts of the Bible are one story written to display God's glory to his people so we might love and worship him.

 Pray for humility and insight before you study God's Word.

GATHER KNOWLEDGE

Read Psalm 1. Look up a definition for the word *blessed*.

What does the blessed person not do?

What does the blessed person do?

Look up a definition for the word *meditate*.

How is the righteous person (the one who is blessed) described in verse 3?

How is the wicked person described in verse 4?

What is the future of the wicked person?

What is the future of the righteous person?

DIGEST THE BIG IDEAS

Why are the contrasting descriptions of the righteous person and the wicked person so effective?

What does the image of the tree show about a person who delights in and meditates on God's Word?

Consider the passage that you read yesterday. Return to your answers or to Deuteronomy 6:1–9. What ideas or principles in the Deuteronomy passage are echoed in Psalm 1?

What is the main idea of Psalm 1?*

What did you learn about God, Jesus Christ, or the gospel from today's study?

*An example main idea can be found on page 131.

GROW IN GODLINESS

How might the main idea of Psalm 1 apply to your circumstances?

Circle the way you will respond to God's Word today.

Today I will...   believe   act   repent   worship   pray

Use this space for your response or to plan how you will respond throughout your day.

Write the verse, attribute of God, or gospel truth you will meditate on today.

Day Four | Grow

Honey is a treat for us, but it's life-giving sustenance for a bee. Once created, it's stored in the comb and doesn't spoil. The Bible holds unchanging truth that will never spoil either. When we have diligently gathered knowledge and digested the big ideas about a passage, we have found a drop of honey that will nourish our souls and produce growth in our lives.

Did you know that a bee's type is determined by its diet? The queen bee is fed a special substance called royal jelly her whole life, while worker bees are fed royal jelly as babies and then switch to a diet of strictly honey and pollen. What the bees consume actually dictates what they become. The same is true for us. When we consume worldly wisdom on the internet or surround ourselves with foolish friends, we will grow more obsessed with the good gifts and the sinful lures of this world. Neither will lead to godliness. But when we consume the life-changing sustenance of God's Word, we become more like our Savior. When God speaks to us through his unchanging Word, it changes us.

In *How to Read the Bible in Changing Times*, professor Mark L. Strauss says, "The Christian life involves not just knowing the Bible's teachings or obeying its commands but walking so close to and so far with God that in each new situation we can identify the heart of God (1 Cor. 2:13–16)."[5] When we have carefully gathered knowledge about the passage we're studying and digested its big ideas, we grow our knowledge of and love for God. He chose to reveal himself through Jesus and through the Bible, so we must pay close attention to God's Word if we want to grow into wise women who can discern God's heart in whatever circumstances we face. Strauss also warns against letting our study of God's Word just be purely academic. It must intersect with our lives and impact our hearts. We start by grasping what the passage meant to the original audience in their time and place, "but listening also means hearing what God is saying to us in our time and place. This must not be just a cognitive exercise; like our love for God, it involves heart, mind, soul, and strength."[6]

God's Word is living and active. When you respond to God's Word, you will be changed by it. As you studied in Psalm 1 yesterday, you will become a strong tree, bearing fruit and standing firm. You become like the people you spend time with, so spend time with Jesus. Studying your Bible builds a relationship with God that causes you to become more like him as you walk in his glorious, perfect presence.

Pray for humility and insight before you study God's Word.

GATHER KNOWLEDGE

Read Psalm 19. Before focusing on verses 7–14, gather knowledge and identify the main idea of verses 1–6 for context. Write every word related to speech and every word related to creation.

Speech

Creation

Fill in the main idea of verses 1–6 below according to what you've read.

God _____ to people through _____ .

Now look at verses 7–9 and fill in the chart by writing the synonym for God's Word found in the verse and writing the benefit in your own words.

VERSE	SYNONYM FOR GOD'S WORD	BENEFIT OF GOD'S WORD
7		
7		
8		
8		
9 *		
9		

Many biblical scholars agree that the fear of the LORD means following the commands of God's Word in this context.

What does David conclude about the benefits of God's Word in verses 10–11?

Verses 12–13 have a different emotion than the verses before them. What is David concerned he'll do?

The words *be acceptable* in verse 14 echo repeated language around sacrifices in the book of Leviticus. Review Psalm 19 and consider these questions: Are these words of David's mouth and this meditation of his heart something that would please God? Why or why not?

DIGEST THE BIG IDEAS

What is different about the descriptions of how God speaks in verses 1–6 and the descriptions of how God speaks in verses 7–11?

How do you think seeing evidence of God in creation is different from learning about him in his Word?

Look back at the benefits of God's Word you wrote in the chart. What words would you use to describe a person who is experiencing those benefits?

Read Psalm 119:9–11. What does the psalmist do with God's Word to receive its benefits?

Read 2 Timothy 3:16–17. What are the benefits of reading God's Word? Star those that are similar to the benefits listed in Psalm 19:7–9.

Read Romans 12:1–2. How is the worship described in these verses similar to the worship described in Psalm 19:14?

What is the main idea of Psalm 19?*

What did you learn about God, Jesus Christ, or the gospel from today's study?

GROW IN GODLINESS

How might the main idea of Psalm 19 apply to your circumstances?

Circle the way you will respond to God's Word today.

Today I will...   believe   act   repent   worship   pray

Use this space for your response or to plan how you will respond throughout your day.

Write the verse, attribute of God, or gospel truth you will meditate on today.

An example main idea can be found on page 131.

Day Five | Enjoy

When I (Gretchen) used to read my Bible, I made it all about myself. I had no plan. I just sat down and randomly opened to any page, hoping to land on an encouraging verse. I had never been taught a better way, never experienced the joy of discovering God through his Word.

But when I was in college, I developed an eating disorder, and in my desperation for healing, I found Jesus. I began studying the Bible to know and love God more and discovered that only God can satisfy the canyon of longing in my heart and that true joy is only found in relationship with him. Instead of opening to random pages, I started reading full books of the Bible and developing an understanding of the big redemption story.

When I started really studying the Word—even on the days I didn't feel like it—I discovered that the more I taste Jesus, the more the rest of the world loses its flavor. As I saw Jesus Christ across the entire story of Scripture, grasping the immensity of what he did for me on the cross, how undeserving I was of his mercy and grace, and the abundant love he lavished on me, I started to enjoy and even crave God's Word.

Too often we expect that delighting in God's Word should come naturally. We wonder if there's something wrong with us when we don't long to open the Scriptures as much as we long to check social media. Rather than the cheap delight of fast food French fries, God's Word offers us daily bread, meals to satisfy and strengthen us, and honey that lingers in our hearts.

We're all hungry for something or someone to delight in, to savor, to enjoy, because we were made to delight in, savor, and enjoy Jesus forever. Every other person or thing eventually disappoints, but Jesus offers us joy in him no matter our circumstances. Christ came full of grace and truth (John 1:14). He came with splendor and majesty, strength and beauty, wisdom and power. The more you gaze upon him in the Word, the more you will be filled with praise and joy.

Enjoying God begins with picking up your spiritual fork and dining at the table of his Word. So if you want to develop joy in God's Word, don't skip the hard parts. Instead, work hard to understand them. Pray for the Holy Spirit to develop your spiritual taste buds so you no longer crave the candy of this world but instead are satisfied by the honey of his Word. When you come to the Word to know God, you'll discover the unshakable joy of relationship with your Savior.

Pray for humility and insight before you study God's Word.

GATHER KNOWLEDGE

Read the following verses and summarize what they say about God's Word.

Deuteronomy 32:47

Psalm 1:1—2

Psalm 119:14—16

Psalm 119:18

Psalm 119:24

Psalm 119:40

Psalm 119:71

Psalm 119.92—93

Psalm 119:103

John 6:66—69

DIGEST THE BIG IDEAS

What themes did you notice in these verses?

Which verse would you choose as the best example of these themes?

What is the main idea of these passages on God's Word?*

What did you learn about God, Jesus Christ, or the gospel from today's study?

GROW IN GODLINESS

How might the main idea of today's reading apply to your circumstances?

Circle the way you will respond to God's Word today.

Today I will...   believe   act   repent   worship   pray

Use this space for your response or to plan how you will respond throughout your day.

Write the verse, attribute of God, or gospel truth you will meditate on today.

*An example main idea can be found on page 131.

Session One Viewer Guide

_____

_____

_____

_____

_____

_____

_____

_____

_____

_____

_____

_____

_____

_____

_____

_____

_____

_____

_____

_____

QUESTIONS FOR DISCUSSION OR REFLECTION

How do you know that God's Word is true and trustworthy?

Why is God's Word the primary source for how we live our lives?

When will you set aside time to do the discipline of completing this Bible study?

The Unchanging Word

Studying the Bible is less like picking up a beach read and more like reading Shakespeare. Before you read his plays, it's best to read a synopsis of what happens and gather knowledge about the context of the time. You might encounter unfamiliar words that you need to look up. When studying Shakespeare, knowing the genre of what you're reading is essential because you'd read a comedy completely differently than you'd approach a tragedy like *Romeo and Juliet*. You might research the themes that scholars agree on before you start reading. And if you don't do these things, you won't enjoy reading Shakespeare—you'll likely be overwhelmed, exhausted, and confused by it.

The Bible is so much greater than a Shakespeare play and infinitely more deserving of special attention than a beach read. Studying and researching before digging into the text might feel strange at first, but building these skills will equip you to study God's Word with confidence and consistency. This week (and next week!), you'll learn more about the gather principle of Bible study. Gathering knowledge about a passage of Scripture begins with asking questions. Researching your questions will help you understand the context of the passage and the basic ideas of what it says before you identify meaning. God's Word never changes, so it can't mean what it never meant. Gathering the details first helps us understand the original meaning, which ultimately helps us enjoy God through his Word.

Day One | Historical Context

In the years I (Maggie) have lived on the farm, my family has had an embarrassing number of cats. The problem is that farms are dangerous and cats are curious—and we all know how the saying goes. If you put a new or unknown object into a cat's environment, they must inspect it, sniffing, pawing, and determining its purpose. My kids often behave the same way, but as humans get older, we tend to lose our curious nature. We wrongly assume that we already understand everything. But to really understand God's Word, we need to be curious—even if (maybe especially if) you grew up in the church or have heard a lot of Bible stories told to you without the language of Scripture.

The Bible was written in a drastically different period in history, so understanding a book or passage's historical context brings the modern reader clarity and understanding. Professors Gordon D. Fee and Douglas Stuart explain that God "chose to speak his eternal truths within the particular circumstances and events of human history."[7] This is why it's essential to begin with gathering knowledge about a passage before you start to determine its meaning. The easiest way to get a full picture of the context of a passage is to be curious, asking who, what, when, where, and why questions.

Historical Context Questions
- When was this book written?
- Who wrote this book? What was their background? What were their circumstances when they wrote the book?
- Who was the original audience of this book? What were their particular circumstances geographically and historically? What were their issues and concerns?
- What was the relationship between the author and the audience?
- Why did the author write this book?

Before you start studying a new book of the Bible, take a day (or more) to study the historical context. Because it's unlikely that you're a biblical scholar, this process requires some outside resources. We highly recommend a study Bible as your primary tool for learning about context, but you can also utilize these free online resources:
- Book summary videos on bibleproject.com
- Commentaries on thegospelcoalition.org
- Introductions to the Bible on blueletterbible.org under the Study tab

Pray for humility and insight before you study God's Word.

GATHER KNOWLEDGE

Over the next few weeks, you'll look at one passage of Scripture, Ephesians 1:1–14, and slowly make your way through the gather, digest, and grow principles. Though you'll only be studying the first fourteen verses of chapter 1, consider reading or listening to all of Ephesians this week to help you grasp the context of the entire book.

Read Ephesians 1:1–14. Who wrote this book?

How does he describe himself?

What do you know about the apostle Paul? If you don't know his background, read Acts 9:1–19.

Read Acts 20:17–38. What news of his anticipated future does Paul give the elders of the church in Ephesus?

Summarize the concerns Paul has for the church in Ephesus.

How would you describe Paul's relationship with the church in Ephesus based on this passage?

Read Ephesians 3:1. What is happening to Paul as he writes this letter to the Ephesians?

Would this have been surprising to the church in Ephesus?

Look at the introduction to Ephesians in a study Bible or use one of the free online resources listed at the start of today's study to answer this question: When was this book written?

DIGEST THE BIG IDEAS

Because you're in the slow knowledge-gathering stage of studying Ephesians 1:1–14 this week, it's best not to skip forward to the big ideas. Instead, you'll answer a question to help you process the connection between the context and the passage in preparation for understanding the big ideas.

Based on what you know about the apostle Paul, why do you think he begins his letter to the Ephesians with the content in Ephesians 1:1–14?

GROW IN GODLINESS

Circle the way you will respond to God's Word today.

Today I will...   believe   act   repent   worship   pray

Use this space for your response or to plan how you will respond throughout your day.

Write the verse, attribute of God, or gospel truth you will meditate on today.

Day Two | Literary Context

The Bible is the inspired, inerrant Word of God. It's breathed out by God and is useful and beneficial for our lives (2 Tim. 3:16–17). The Bible contains sixty-six books written by a variety of authors in multiple languages. Authors Tim Challies and Josh Byers explain, "God ordained and oversaw the personality of the authors, their circumstances, their style, their training, and their process of writing to bring about his Word. The human authors were really writing, and God was really breathing."[8]

The sixty-six books of the Bible were agreed upon over time by several councils in the first century A.D. The books of the Bible aren't ordered chronologically but are grouped by genre, a category of literature based on subject, form, or style.[9] As you gather knowledge about the passage or book you're studying, it's essential to consider the genre and literary style, which together make up the literary context.

All genres have unique characteristics that set them apart and help us understand what to expect and what the author is trying to say. Just imagine what would happen if you tried to read *The Chronicles of Narnia* like a history textbook or if you tried to read a poem as if it were a newspaper article. It just wouldn't work, or even worse, you might come to some really strange conclusions.

The primarily Jewish original audience of the Bible would have had working knowledge of the basic elements of the different genres, just like we generally know what to expect from a romantic comedy, historical fiction, or murder mystery movie. But because we aren't the original audience, we have to put in a little work to learn and recall the elements of each biblical genre.

Day Three and Day Four this week will cover the genres of the Old and New Testaments, highlighting important questions to ask the text and different literary styles you might encounter within that genre. These days will give you a basic framework, but know that you can use a study Bible and the recommended Bible resources from yesterday to aid you in discerning genre elements and literary styles as you study. As you grow in your comfort with each genre, you'll begin to recognize their elements and when an author changes literary styles within the genre on your own.

Pray for humility and insight before you study God's Word.

GATHER KNOWLEDGE

You'll continue with literary context tomorrow, but for today, your Bible study work is to continue uncovering the historical context of the book of Ephesians. Consider reading or listening to all of Ephesians this week to help you do so.

Read Ephesians 1:1–14. Who is the original audience? How does Paul describe them?

Read Acts 18:18–21 and summarize Paul's first short visit to Ephesus.

Read Acts 18:24–28. What happens in Ephesus to lead some people to have an incomplete understanding of the gospel?

Read the following passages and list two to four important details you learn about the people of Ephesus.

    Acts 19:1–7

    Acts 19:8–10

Acts 19:11—20

Acts 19:21—20:1

Read a description of the ancient city of Ephesus from the introduction to Ephesians in a study Bible or use one of the free resources listed in yesterday's study. Note any important details you learn about Ephesus that you hadn't already gleaned from Acts 19.

DIGEST THE BIG IDEAS

Based on what you learned about the church in Ephesus, what parts of Ephesians 1:1—14 may have been particularly important for them to grasp? Why?

GROW IN GODLINESS

Circle the way you will respond to God's Word today.

Today I will...   believe   act   repent   worship   pray

Use this space for your response or to plan how you will respond throughout your day.

Write the verse, attribute of God, or gospel truth you will meditate on today.

Day Three | Old Testament Genres

THE PENTATEUCH				
GENESIS	EXODUS	LEVITICUS	NUMBERS	DEUTERONOMY

The first five books of the Bible are called the Pentateuch. These books were primarily written by Moses as the Israelites prepared to enter the promised land of Canaan. They describe God's creation of the world, his relationship to his people, the history of the patriarchs and founding stories of Israel, and God's righteous laws (including the Ten Commandments and the sacrificial system). These books lay a foundation for God's plan of salvation to be fulfilled in Jesus Christ by establishing his covenant promises to his people despite their sinful rebellion. The Pentateuch reveals humanity's need for a Savior—Jesus Christ, who came to fulfill the law (Matt. 5:17) and restore right relationship with the one true God.

Questions for Studying the Pentateuch
- What does this passage say about God's covenant with his people?
- Why would this story have been important to the original audience of Israelites entering the promised land of Canaan?
- How does this law set God's people apart as holy?

Literary Styles: narrative, laws, songs, speeches

OLD TESTAMENT HISTORY						
JOSHUA	JUDGES	RUTH	1 SAMUEL	2 SAMUEL	1 KINGS	2 KINGS
1 CHRONICLES		2 CHRONICLES		EZRA	NEHEMIAH	ESTHER

The Old Testament history books detail Israel's history and all have settings, characters, and plots. Remember that these history books aren't exhaustive. Each story is included to teach you something about the salvation story and God's nature and purposes. The history books tell real stories about real people living in a broken world. They help us understand how God works in relationship with his people and how to live under God's kind and sovereign rule.[10]

Questions for Studying Old Testament History
- Who are the people in this passage? What else do you know about these people from the rest of the Bible?
- What is the setting of this passage?

- What are the major plot points and the climax of this passage?
- What does this passage say about God's covenant with his people?

Literary Styles: narrative, songs, speeches

WISDOM AND POETRY				
JOB	PSALMS	PROVERBS	ECCLESIASTES	SONG OF SOLOMON

The wisdom and poetry books of the Bible express the broad array of human emotions in light of God's consistent character and faithfulness and include biblical principles for how to live. Job, Proverbs, Ecclesiastes, and Song of Solomon are wisdom literature. They address many of life's questions, struggles, and doubts. The book of Psalms includes songs of lament, praise, wisdom, confession, messianic prophecy, and thanksgiving. The psalms express ways to communicate with God and the nature of his character. Both wisdom literature and poetry reveal who God is and what it looks like to live in relationship with him. Know that the biblical wisdom included in these books is descriptive rather than prescriptive—general rather than universal truths that are meant to point us to the holiness of God and call us to live in light of who he is.[11]

Questions for Studying Wisdom and Poetry
- What poetic elements are used in this passage?
- How does this passage describe a godly life?
- What emotions is the author expressing?
- What truths about God is the author preaching to their emotions and circumstances?

Literary Styles: poetry, songs, lament, confession, thanksgiving, proverbs, parallelism, instruction, narrative, figurative language

PROPHECY					
ISAIAH	JEREMIAH	LAMENTATIONS	EZEKIEL*	DANIEL*	HOSEA
JOEL	AMOS	OBADIAH	JONAH	MICAH	NAHUM
HABAKKUK	ZEPHANIAH	HAGGAI		ZECHARIAH*	MALACHI

The Old Testament prophets were sent by God to proclaim his message to the nation of Israel. This message was a declaration of God's covenant faithfulness and a call to repent and return to him before impending judgment. Prophets also foretold the future, including the coming of Christ. Before studying a book of Old Testament prophecy, research any context you can find in a corresponding Old Testament history book like 1 and 2 Kings or 1 and

---

The second half of the book of Daniel and smaller portions of Ezekiel and Zechariah are apocalyptic literature.

2 Chronicles. The core of God's message is the same throughout all Old Testament prophecy: though God's people had forsaken his law and his ways, God had been, was, and always would be faithful to his covenant, an anchor of hope for every heart.

Questions for Studying Prophecy

- Who is speaking in this passage?
- What is happening in Israel at the time of this prophecy?
- What is the purpose of this judgment?
- What glimpses of hope are offered?

Literary Styles: poetry, lament, oracles, narrative, apocalyptic prophecy

 Pray for humility and insight before you study God's Word.

GATHER KNOWLEDGE

Today you'll begin discerning the literary context of Ephesians. Consider reading or listening to all of Ephesians this week.

Read Ephesians 1:1–14. Now watch the Book of Ephesians Summary video by the BibleProject at bibleproject.com/explore/video/ephesians/. What are the main themes of the book of Ephesians?

What is the primary purpose or message of the book of Ephesians?

What are the two main sections of the book of Ephesians?

What details are mentioned in the video about Ephesians 1:1–14?

DIGEST THE BIG IDEAS

What role or purpose does Ephesians 1:1–14 play in the larger message of the book of Ephesians?

GROW IN GODLINESS

Circle the way you will respond to God's Word today.

Today I will...   believe   act   repent   worship   pray

Use this space for your response or to plan how you will respond throughout your day.

Write the verse, attribute of God, or gospel truth you will meditate on today.

Day Four | New Testament Genres

THE GOSPELS			
MATTHEW	MARK	LUKE	JOHN

Though the Gospels focus on different aspects of the same accounts, the message is all the same: Jesus Christ is the promised Messiah, the Son of God, who came to earth to fulfill the law, die in the place of sinners, and grant eternal life to those who trust in him for salvation. As you study the Gospels, keep your eyes open for ways in which Jesus fulfilled the promises of the Old Testament. Matthew, Mark, and Luke are known as the Synoptic Gospels because they follow a similar structure and contain many of the same stories and information. John's Gospel is different in style and structure, containing many details and stories not covered in the other three Gospels. Each Gospel writer chose specific details according to their specific audience and purpose for writing the book. Before you study a Gospel, seek to understand its unique elements and watch to see how the author fulfills that purpose to show you a unique facet of the life of Jesus.

Questions for Studying the Gospels
- What is the background of the author?
- Who is Jesus speaking to? What underlying motives might he be addressing?
- How does Jesus interact differently with various types of people?
- What literary style is Jesus using? How does that inform the meaning of what he's saying?

Literary Styles: biographical narrative, dialogue, sermons, parables, hyperbole, metaphors

NEW TESTAMENT HISTORY
ACTS

The book of Acts is a historical narrative detailing the foundation of the church following the resurrection of Jesus Christ. It's often considered a continuation of the book of Luke, but it follows a different structure from the Gospels. This book provides important historical background for many of the epistles. As you study Acts, remember that it's not prescriptive instruction on how to do church but rather historical accounts that "teach the nature, mission, power, and potential of the church."[12]

Questions for Studying Acts
- Who is in this passage? What do you already know about them?
- How is the Holy Spirit active in this passage?

- What happens to God's people in this passage?
- What principles for the church are in this passage?
- What details about the gospel are in this passage?

Literary Styles: narrative, dialogue, sermons

EPISTLES				
ROMANS	1 CORINTHIANS	2 CORINTHIANS	GALATIANS	EPHESIANS
PHILIPPIANS	COLOSSIANS		1 THESSALONIANS	2 THESSALONIANS
1 TIMOTHY	2 TIMOTHY	TITUS	PHILEMON	HEBREWS
JAMES	1 PETER	2 PETER	1 JOHN	2 JOHN	3 JOHN	JUDE

The New Testament epistles (or letters) were written to instruct, encourage, and exhort the early church. These letters were composed with specific purposes by particular authors to certain groups of people. They all follow a similar structure, beginning with a greeting, followed by the author's purpose for writing and his teaching, and concluding with a benediction. Originally these letters were read publicly in the church body when they were received. As you study each epistle, notice the author's purpose for the original audience. The shorter length combined with the theological depth of each epistle requires repetitive, slow, and careful reading. Just as a bee must burrow into flowers to suck out nectar, dig into specific themes and immerse yourself in the author's progression of arguments. When you face a particularly difficult theological passage, let Scripture interpret Scripture, beginning with other passages from the book you're studying, then broadening out to other books written by the same author, and then broadening out to the Bible as a whole.

Questions for Studying Epistles
- Who is the author? Who is the audience? What interactions have they had in the past?
- What part of the letter is this?
- How does this passage relate to the Old Testament?
- Is this a statement of fact, command, or principle?
- How does this passage further explain Jesus' life, death, and resurrection?

Literary Styles: letter, thanksgiving and praise, prayers, songs, indicatives (statements of fact), imperatives (commands), wisdom, Old Testament quotations

The book of Revelation reveals Christ and his past, present, and future rule and reign.[13] It looks ahead to the consummation of God's kingdom, when all will be made right through Christ's return, his final triumph over evil and Satan, and his eternal reign. It highlights and proclaims God as the central figure of all history—the Alpha and the Omega, the Faithful God, the One who was and is and is to come.[14] Before you study Revelation, it's helpful to study the book of Daniel because Revelation often alludes to the apocalyptic prophecy in the second half of that book. As you study, keep in mind the symbolic nature of Revelation and resist the temptation to compare it to today's circumstances and crises. Don't aim to understand or interpret every image. Instead, seek to identify the principles displayed through the imagery and symbolism. Revelation reveals that God has always been in control and that he always will be. He will restore all broken things and redeem them for his glory, and we will live in perfect, unbroken fellowship with him for all eternity!

Questions for Studying Apocalyptic Literature
- What does this image demonstrate about God, the world, or humanity?
- Who is the original audience and what did this mean to them?
- How does this passage fit within the context of the earlier chapters of this book?

Literary Styles: letter, apocalyptic prophecy, imagery, symbolism, metaphor

 Pray for humility and insight before you study God's Word.

GATHER KNOWLEDGE

Consider reading or listening to all of Ephesians this week to gain literary context.

Read Ephesians 1:1–14. What part of the letter is this?

What word is repeated three times in verse 3? What literary style is this passage written in based on this clue?

Verses 3–14 are one long sentence in the original Greek language. Do you think this sentence is a statement of fact or a command? Why?

List any Old Testament images or concepts you notice.

DIGEST THE BIG IDEAS

What emotion is prevalent in this passage?

What response do you think Paul is aiming to create in the hearts of the Ephesians?

GROW IN GODLINESS

Circle the way you will respond to God's Word today.

Today I will...   believe   act   repent   worship   pray

Use this space for your response or to plan how you will respond throughout your day.

Write the verse, attribute of God, or gospel truth you will meditate on today.

Day Five | Pay Attention

I (Maggie) used to love watching police procedural TV shows. I still love a cozy mystery novel and, yes, I'll admit, a well-done true crime documentary or podcast. I relish solving the puzzle as the story unfolds and watching the bad guy be brought to justice. Ultimately, these genres are all about paying attention to the details, like the personalities and interactions of the people involved, but always first to the crime scene itself.

God has given us all the details we need to digest the big ideas of a passage of Scripture, if we will pay close attention to them. We won't always be able to identify the precise meaning of every detail, but we can learn to see how the details come together to explain the mysteries of God's will revealed in Christ Jesus (Eph. 1:8–9).

You've spent the week learning how to discover details about a text by being curious and asking questions. Today, we'll cover some other methods for gathering knowledge. Some people like to do this portion of their study by printing out a double-spaced copy of the passage, some like to jot down details in a journal, and some simply do it right in their Bibles. Try different methods to find what works best for you.

Notice repetition. It's easiest to notice repetition by reading the passage repeatedly or out loud. Once you've identified a repeated word, look again to see if there are any other words that mean essentially the same thing (synonyms) in the passage. Either mark these words in the text or make a list of them.

Look up definitions. Which words would you struggle to explain to a child? Look up definitions for them (preferably in a Bible dictionary—you can see our recommendation on page 130) and note any details that stand out to you. If there are complicated theological terms, look them up even if you think you already know their meaning.

Identify transition words. Look for connecting words and phrases like *therefore, and, but, for this reason, according to, so, now,* and others. In narratives, pay attention to words that denote the passing of time. Ask yourself how the connecting and time-related words show the relationship between the concepts explained in the passage or the elements of the plot.

Summarize, paraphrase, or write an outline. Generally, you'll feel more comfortable with one of these reading comprehension methods than the others. Start this practice where you already feel comfortable, then challenge yourself to break out and try developing new skills in this area. I (Maggie) prefer to summarize by using bullet points (especially when reading narrative), but paraphrasing helps me identify words and concepts I don't fully understand and writing an outline is helpful when trying to follow an author's argument.

Remember: you don't have to do any of this perfectly. No one is going to grade your Bible study. The point is never perfection. Following the principles of Bible study will give you confidence in your interpretation of God's Word. As you deepen your understanding of the Bible, you'll see God's unchanging character more clearly and grow to enjoy and love him more.

Pray for humility and insight before you study God's Word.

GATHER KNOWLEDGE

Read Ephesians 1:1–14. Write down any repeated words and concepts.

Look up definitions for words you aren't familiar with or complicated theological terms like *predestined*, *adoption*, *redemption*, and *inheritance*. Take notes on anything that stands out to you.

Write down any transition words and what verses they occur in.

Summarize, paraphrase, or write an outline of this passage.

DIGEST THE BIG IDEAS

Look back at any repetition you noticed. Why might Paul be drawing attention to these concepts? Write a summary of what he says about each repeated concept.

What themes or details are standing out to you based on what you observed about the text? You'll come back to these as you make your final assessment of the main idea on Week Four Day Two.

GROW IN GODLINESS

Circle the way you will respond to God's Word today.

Today I will...   believe   act   repent   worship   pray

Use this space for your response or to plan how you will respond throughout your day.

Write the verse, attribute of God, or gospel truth you will meditate on today.

Session Two Viewer Guide

_____
_____
_____
_____
_____
_____
_____
_____
_____
_____
_____
_____
_____
_____
_____
_____
_____
_____
_____

QUESTIONS FOR DISCUSSION OR REFLECTION

Consider one of your closest relationships. How do you invest in that relationship?

What does your life look like when you're in a season of not investing in your relationship with God through his Word?

What does your life look like when you are investing in your relationship with God through his Word?

WEEK THREE

The Good News of the Word

You probably didn't realize at the start of this study that you'd not only be learning about enjoying God through his Word but also about bees. As we've researched bees, we've been surprised by how little scientists actually know about these incredible insects. Often, scientists are only making informed guesses about why bees do what they do—like the activity of forming themselves into a chain, called festooning. Some theories speculate that it's for measuring space, some for forming or softening wax, and others for creating a scaffolding to build honeycombs.[15] There's plenty of evidence for each theory, but none explain it completely, so maybe scientists have missed the point altogether. The same can be true of Bible study. We focus so hard on the details of each verse that we sometimes miss the bigger picture—the chain of redemption that links all of the Bible together into one story.

The first time I (Gretchen) read through the entire Bible, I was in awe of God's work of redemption. My faith was strengthened, my passion was sparked, and my desire to share the hope of the gospel was stirred. Reading the Bible from start to finish helped me to better grasp the overarching narrative, the consistency of God's character, the power of the gospel of Jesus Christ, and the threads of hope woven in every book. It helped me see that the Bible is a book about God, breathed out by the Creator of the universe, yet written by humans inspired by the Holy Spirit (2 Tim. 3:16–17; 2 Pet. 1:21). The Bible is one story showcasing God's glory.

This week focuses on understanding the big story of the Bible and how the Bible fits together to tell one story of God's redemption of his people. You might hear this big story of the Bible referred to as the metanarrative of Scripture, but we'll refer to it as the Bible's redemption story because it demonstrates how God has always been working to rescue and redeem his people.

God's redemption story has four parts: creation, fall, redemption, and consummation. When you identify where the passage falls on the timeline of redemptive history, you are gathering knowledge about its context. But the four parts also establish the pattern of God's redemption story, which is repeated in smaller narratives throughout Scripture. So as you see the patterns of creation, fall, redemption, and consummation throughout the Bible, you're also beginning to digest the big ideas of the text.

The redemption story of the Bible is the gospel story, and the climax is Jesus' life, death, and resurrection. We are still living in this portion of the redemption story—Christ has already come, but we are still awaiting the final consummation of redemption. As we study God's Word, we sit at a unique vantage point. We can look back and see how God was always on a mission to rescue and redeem his people, and we can look forward to the final act of the story. [16]

Day One | Creation

God created the world and called it good and even made it good for us. Being in nature or just looking out the window at a beautiful scene reduces stress and boosts our happiness hormones. Gazing at unending ocean waves or standing at the edge of the immense Grand Canyon moves our souls. God's creation echoes his character. It shows us that he is great and mighty and that we are insufficient and dependent. He is all-powerful and we are needy. He is eternal and we are from dust and to dust we will return. And all this recognizing of God's greatness is good for our souls. We are made in his image, but we are not God.

The Bible begins by introducing the main character of the entire story: God. God is from everlasting to everlasting, existing outside of time and space as three persons in one being: the Father, Son, and Holy Spirit. God is the Creator of all things, the One around whom all things revolve, the Sustainer of life, the Author of existence. God created everything from nothing—the earth, the heavens, the waters, land, seas, and all animals and birds. Finally, he created man and woman in his own image to reflect his glory and enjoy relationship with him. God declared all his creation very good (Gen. 1:27, 31). Adam and Eve were naked and unashamed, living in the garden as cultivators and children of God.

God's story begins (and ends) with a world that is perfectly good. God created a perfectly right world because he is perfectly righteous. The biblical pattern of creation is often displayed in God's rule and authority over all of creation. From God's sovereignty over when a baby is born to the miracles that Jesus performed that defied all science, God is in charge. He created the world, and he holds it together. Occasionally you'll see glimpses of the way things were in the garden of Eden—humans cultivating the ground and subduing animals or walking closely with God or bearing God's image. So while the storyline of creation is contained in Genesis 1–2, don't miss the pattern of creation throughout the Bible.

Redemptive History Timeline

CREATION	FALL	REDEMPTION		CONSUMMATION
Genesis 1–2	Genesis 3	Genesis 4–John ✝	Acts–Jude	Revelation

Questions to Identify the Biblical Pattern of Creation
- How is God's rule and authority as sovereign Creator evident?
- How are people fulfilling or abdicating their roles as cultivators and caretakers of creation?
- How are people bearing the image of God or not?

Pray for humility and insight before you study God's Word.

GATHER KNOWLEDGE

Today's Bible study will help you identify the main elements of creation.

Read Genesis 1. What words and phrases are repeated throughout? (Note that there are a lot, but you don't have to get every single one.)

What do you think is the purpose of this repetition?

In verses 26–31, the pattern is no longer followed. What do you think is the significance of this break in the repetition?

Look at verses 26–27. What is special about the way God creates man and woman?

Look at verses 26 and 28. How are people to interact with creation?

What is God's final pronouncement about creation in verse 31?

DIGEST THE BIG IDEAS

Read Genesis 1:1–2 along with John 1:1–3. Our God exists in three persons (also called the Trinity)—the Father, the Son (Jesus Christ or the Word), and the Holy Spirit. Which persons of the Trinity are involved in the act of creation?

Read Colossians 1:15–17 and Hebrews 1:3. What is Jesus Christ's continued role in creation?

What involvement do people have in creating and sustaining the world according to what you've just read?

What is the main idea of Genesis 1?*

What did you learn about God, Jesus Christ, or the gospel from today's study?

GROW IN GODLINESS

How might the main idea of Genesis 1 apply to your circumstances?

An example main idea can be found on page 131.

Circle the way you will respond to God's Word today.

Today I will...   believe   act   repent   worship   pray

Use this space for your response or to plan how you will respond throughout your day.

Write the verse, attribute of God, or gospel truth you will meditate on today.

Day Two | Fall

My (Maggie's) family lives on a small hobby farm. We have horses, cows, the sweetest donkey, and a small herd of fainting goats. I guess we've taken God's call to Adam and Eve to have dominion over the animals a bit literally. But being a farmer in a fallen world is hard. For each year we've had goats, we've also seen one die. Each of these unpreventable deaths is another stark reminder that we live in a broken world. As our family huddles together and grieves each loss, I remind my three boys: *It's not supposed to be this way.* Because of the fall, sin entered the world and brought brokenness to our hearts and to all of creation.

The saddest section of the redemption story of the Bible is the fall. In Genesis 3, Eve listened to the deceitful lies of Satan (who appeared as a serpent) and believed that God had withheld good from her and Adam. She desired what God had forbidden—to eat from the tree of the knowledge of good and evil. Her longing to be like God conceived disobedience. When Eve and Adam both ate the forbidden fruit, their eyes were opened, they realized they were naked, and they hid from God. Sin brought about the death, shame, and depravity that every human experiences.

The biblical pattern of the fall throughout the Bible is that while humans still bear the image of God, they also inherit the sin nature of Adam. We are children of disobedience and have sinned and fall short of the glory of God (Eph. 2:2; Rom. 3:23). Our hearts are no longer oriented toward God and neighbor but toward self. The fall distorted our desires, rewired our hearts, and separated us from the original unhindered fellowship with God that Adam and Eve experienced in the garden of Eden. Because the wages of sin is death (Rom. 6:23), we live under the curse and power of sin, in dire need of deliverance—as witnessed throughout the Israelites' repeated rebellion against God's words, ways, and will. Unless God intervenes, every person is under the punishment of sin and deserves the just wrath of God for disobedience. While the events of the fall are documented in Genesis 3, you'll see the pattern and effects of the fall displayed throughout the rest of the Bible.

Redemptive History Timeline

CREATION	FALL	REDEMPTION		CONSUMMATION
Genesis 1–2	Genesis 3	Genesis 4–John	✝ Acts–Jude	Revelation

Questions to Identify the Biblical Pattern of the Fall

- How is humanity's sinfulness or rebellion against God's rule evident?
- Are there any elements of the brokenness of creation?
- How is God's judgment handled in this passage?

Pray for humility and insight before you study God's Word.

GATHER KNOWLEDGE

Read Genesis 3. Look closely at verses 1–13 and note the actions of each character.

   The serpent (Satan)

   The woman (later named Eve)

   Adam

   God

Look at verses 14–19. What consequences are given to each character?

   The serpent (Satan)

   The woman (later named Eve)

   Adam

   Creation

Look at verse 21. What does God do for Adam and Eve? Do you see any foreshadowing of how God will cover sins in the future? If not, come back to this question after you complete tomorrow's study.

DIGEST THE BIG IDEAS

Read Romans 1:21–25. What is humanity's deepest problem?

What similarities do you see between this description in Romans and Eve's motivation to take and eat the fruit in Genesis 3:5–6?

Read Romans 3:23. What is the problem of all people?

Read Hebrews 2:14–15. How was the hope of Genesis 3:15 fulfilled in Jesus Christ?

What is the main idea of Genesis 3?*

What did you learn about God, Jesus Christ, or the gospel from today's study?

*An example main idea can be found on page 131.

GROW IN GODLINESS

How might the main idea of Genesis 3 apply to your circumstances?

Circle the way you will respond to God's Word today.

Today I will...   believe   act   repent   worship   pray

Use this space for your response or to plan how you will respond throughout your day.

Write the verse, attribute of God, or gospel truth you will meditate on today.

Day Three | Redemption

My (Maggie's) grandpa was a redeemer. Well, he was a garbage collector in the days before thrift stores existed when almost everything unwanted went in the trash. He lived with an unwavering belief that nothing of value should be thrown away because it might serve its purpose someday. He must have saved thousands of items from the garbage dump. I personally own and use dozens of his dump finds in my everyday life—for example, the antique desk where I'm currently sitting and the shoe shelf in my mudroom. Grandpa was a rescuer and redeemer at heart, bearing God's image and unwittingly displaying God's pattern of redemption for countless years before he finally accepted Christ as his Redeemer on his deathbed.

Yesterday you faced the ugly truth of our fallen state without Christ, but praise God for being a Redeemer! While Satan aimed to destroy God's good creation and his people, God had—and always has—a greater plan to rescue his people and restore their purpose. Redemption is God's miraculous work of grace to save his people from sin's dominion and make them his own.

Old Testament history is full of images of redemption and God's unfolding plan to redeem his people through Jesus Christ's death and resurrection. God promised a Savior would one day come to crush the serpent, establishing a foundation of hope that unites all of Scripture (Gen. 3:15). God rescued Noah's family in the ark from his judgment (Gen. 6–8). Then God called Abram from among the nations and promised to make him a nation through which all the earth would be blessed (Gen. 12). Through Moses, God redeemed his people from slavery and brought them through the waters of the Red Sea to deliverance (Ex. 12–14). Then through Moses, God entered into covenant with the Israelites and gave them his law to relate to him and to set them apart from the nations (Ex. 19–24). God instituted the sacrificial system to temporarily atone for sin. God's people needed a Savior, a mediator to come and rescue them from their cyclical rebellion. God sent the prophets to declare this message to the Israelites, pointing them back to the covenant and calling them to repent of their sin and live by faith in him.

Thousands of years after the initial promise of redemption, God sent the promised Savior: Jesus Christ. The New Testament tells the story of new covenant life in him. Jesus came to earth to live a perfect life, call people to repent and believe, and die on the cross as the perfect sacrifice for our sins (Mark 1:15; Heb. 10:10). Jesus Christ fulfilled the law of God revealed in the Old Testament (Matt. 5:17), releasing sinners from its demands when they trust in him for forgiveness of their sins. On the cross, Jesus bore the wrath of God for his chosen people and rose again so they could be freed from sin's tyranny and death to new life in Christ (Isa. 53:5–6; Rom. 5:9; 2 Cor. 5:17).

Under the new covenant inaugurated by the death and resurrection of Jesus Christ, children of God are given the Holy Spirit to transform them to become more like Christ and empower them to live for God's glory (Rom. 8:16;

2 Cor. 3:18). God's redeemed people now live in fellowship as his church, following God's commands to go and make disciples of all nations and to love God and their neighbor (Matt. 28:19–20; Mark 12:29–31).

The biblical pattern of redemption offers glimpses of Jesus Christ and the redemption he purchased on the cross throughout both the Old and New Testaments. When identifying elements of redemption in a passage, pay attention to the things that show the people's desperate need for a Savior. You'll come back to this concept in Week Four when we cover seeing Jesus Christ in all of Scripture.

Redemptive History Timeline

CREATION	FALL	REDEMPTION		CONSUMMATION
Genesis 1–2	Genesis 3	Genesis 4–John	Acts–Jude	Revelation

Questions to Identify the Biblical Pattern of Redemption
- Who needs rescue? Who is providing rescue?
- Are there any promises made or needs highlighted that can only be fulfilled or resolved by a Savior?
- Are the people this text is written to living under the old or new covenant? How does that impact their relationship with God?

 Pray for humility and insight before you study God's Word.

GATHER KNOWLEDGE

Read John 19:16–37 and summarize what happens in two or three sentences.

Look at verses 16–22. What do the chief priests argue with Pilate about? What does this show about the attitude of the Jewish leaders toward Jesus?

What phrase is repeated in verses 24, 28, and 36?

What final words does Jesus declare just before his death? What do you think the "it" refers to?

Read Luke 24:1–12 and summarize what happens in two or three sentences.

What had Jesus prophesied about himself according to verses 6–7? (You can read this account in Luke 9:22.)

DIGEST THE BIG IDEAS

What does it prove that Jesus' death and resurrection fulfilled what was written in the Old Testament and what Jesus said about himself?

Read Ephesians 1:7–8. What was accomplished through Jesus' death on the cross?

Read Ephesians 2:4–8. What was accomplished through the grace offered by Jesus' death and resurrection? How are people saved?

Read Colossians 1:13–14. How do these verses describe what Jesus accomplished through his death and resurrection?

What is the main idea of these passages on the death and resurrection of Jesus?*

An example main idea can be found on page 131.

What did you learn about God, Jesus Christ, or the gospel from today's study?

GROW IN GODLINESS

How might the main idea of today's reading apply to your circumstances?

Circle the way you will respond to God's Word today.

Today I will...   believe   act   repent   worship   pray

Use this space for your response or to plan how you will respond throughout your day.

Write the verse, attribute of God, or gospel truth you will meditate on today.

Day Four | Consummation

Poet and hymn writer Fanny Crosby became blind at just two months old when a simple infection was mistreated by a doctor. Her father died soon after, forcing her mother to find work and leaving Fanny to be raised by her grandmother. Despite the hardships she faced as a young girl, Fanny developed a love for poetry and stringing words together like pearls. Throughout her life, Fanny wrote over nine thousand hymns, including the beloved hymn "Take the World but Give Me Jesus."[17] The last stanza of this hymn reads:

> Take the world, but give me Jesus;
> in his cross my trust shall be
> till with clearer, brighter vision
> face to face my Lord I see.[18]

Although her physical eyes couldn't see, the eyes of Fanny's heart saw Christ, and she longed to see his face when she entered her eternal home in God's presence.

Since the ascension of Jesus Christ after his resurrection, believers like Fanny look forward to the day when he will come again to fully establish the kingdom of God. The book of Revelation reveals the consummation, the final fulfillment of all God's purposes. Jesus Christ will come again and Satan will be destroyed finally and forever (Rev. 20:10). God will make all things new, including a new heaven and new earth where his servants—those whose names are written in the Lamb's book of life because they were redeemed through the death and resurrection of Jesus Christ—will dwell (Rev. 21–22). When he returns, Jesus will establish his visible rule and God will dwell with his people again. For now, believers live with steadfast hope in Jesus' final victory and their eternal future in his presence.

The biblical pattern of the final consummation of all God's plans and promises is most evident in the theme of hope throughout the Bible. All believers—those in the Old Testament, New Testament, and today—put their hope for salvation in the person and work of Jesus Christ. We also look forward further still to an eternal future, where sin and pain and death are no more and we joyfully worship God in his presence.

Redemptive History Timeline

CREATION	FALL	REDEMPTION		CONSUMMATION
Genesis 1–2	Genesis 3	Genesis 4–John ✝	Acts–Jude	Revelation

Questions to Identify the Biblical Pattern of Consummation

- How is God currently dwelling with his people?
- Are the people of God at home? Why or why not?
- What are God's people placing their hope in?
- Are there any promises that won't be fulfilled until Christ comes again?

 Pray for humility and insight before you study God's Word.

GATHER KNOWLEDGE

Read Revelation 21:1–8 and Revelation 21:22–22:5. What words of hope does God proclaim in Revelation 21:5?

Describe the physical details of the new heaven and new earth. What will be completely redeemed according to these descriptions?

Describe the emotional and spiritual state of those who will dwell in the new heaven and new earth (21:4; 22:3–5).

Where will God live (21:3)?

Read Revelation 19:11, 13, 16 and Revelation 21:6, 22. Write down all the names of God mentioned.

DIGEST THE BIG IDEAS

How do the names of God in Revelation 19 and 21 offer hope?

How does God's future dwelling place offer hope to his people still living in a broken world?

Read Hebrews 11:13–16. What future hope did the people described in Hebrews 11 (the chapter of the Bible called the Hall of Faith) put their trust in?

Read 1 Peter 1:3–5. Describe the hope of believers. How do believers receive this hope? How is it secured?

What is the main idea of these passages on the consummation?*

What did you learn about God, Jesus Christ, or the gospel from today's study?

An example main idea can be found on page 131.

GROW IN GODLINESS

How might the main idea of today's reading apply to your circumstances?

Circle the way you will respond to God's Word today.

Today I will...   believe   act   repent   worship   pray

Use this space for your response or to plan how you will respond throughout your day.

Write the verse, attribute of God, or gospel truth you will meditate on today.

Day Five | Patterns of the Redemption Story

We hope that at this point, you can confidently identify where a book of the Bible falls on the timeline of redemptive history. Gathering this knowledge gives you the context necessary to understand what a passage of Scripture meant to its original audience. But the parts of the redemption story also demonstrate the biblical pattern of how God redeems his people. Remember: recognizing these patterns is more than just gathering knowledge—it's the beginning of the digestion process. The patterns of creation, fall, redemption, and consummation throughout the Bible point to God's gospel plan. In the Old Testament, they were signs to the people of what God's rescue and rule would look like. They laid the groundwork for the redemption that would be offered in Jesus' life, death, and resurrection. The patterns of creation, fall, redemption, and consummation echo through the New Testament books, calling out the good news of the gospel—Jesus Christ has come, and he is coming again.

Like a bee that has flittered from flower to flower to gather nectar and fill its honey stomach, we hope you're filled with knowledge about Ephesians 1:1–14 from your Bible study in Week Two and are ready to start digesting it into honey today as you identify the patterns of the redemption story in the passage.

 Pray for humility and insight before you study God's Word.

GATHER KNOWLEDGE

Read Ephesians 1:1–14. Which period of the redemption story you studied this week does the book of Ephesians take place during? Put a star in the correct place on the timeline.

CREATION	FALL	REDEMPTION		CONSUMMATION
Genesis 1–2	Genesis 3	Genesis 4–John	✝ Acts–Jude	Revelation

What are some of the important elements of that part of the redemption story?

Which of those elements are evident in this passage?

DIGEST THE BIG IDEAS

Choose one of these questions to answer about the pattern of creation displayed in Ephesians 1:1–14.

• How is God's rule and authority as sovereign Creator evident?

• How are people fulfilling or abdicating their roles as cultivators and caretakers of creation?

• How are people bearing the image of God or not?

Choose one of these questions to answer about the pattern of the fall displayed in Ephesians 1:1–14.

• How is humanity's sinfulness or rebellion against God's rule evident?

• Are there any elements of the brokenness of creation?

• How is God's judgment handled in this passage?

Choose one of these questions to answer about the pattern of redemption displayed in Ephesians 1:1–14.

• Who needs rescue? Who is providing rescue?

• Are there any promises made or needs highlighted that can only be fulfilled or resolved by a Savior?

• Are the people this text is written to living under the old or new covenant? How does that impact their relationship with God?

Choose one of these questions to answer about the pattern of consummation displayed in Ephesians 1:1–14.

• How is God currently dwelling with his people?

• Are the people of God at home? Why or why not?

• What are God's people placing their hope in?

• Are there any promises that won't be fulfilled until Christ comes again?

The patterns of the redemption story that you learned to identify this week help you see the threads of the gospel that are woven throughout all of the Bible. Identifying these gospel threads is one way to discover more about the gospel in any passage you're studying. Consider responding with these redemption story patterns when you answer the next question today and in future days of study.

What did you learn about God, Jesus Christ, or the gospel from today's study?

GROW IN GODLINESS

Circle the way you will respond to God's Word today.

Today I will...   believe   act   repent   worship   pray

Use this space for your response or to plan how you will respond throughout your day.

Write the verse, attribute of God, or gospel truth you will meditate on today.

Session Three Viewer Guide

_____
_____
_____
_____
_____
_____
_____
_____
_____
_____
_____
_____
_____
_____
_____
_____
_____
_____
_____
_____

QUESTIONS FOR DISCUSSION OR REFLECTION

What reminds you of the goodness of God's creation?

Where have you seen the effects of the fall in your life lately?

What hard or painful circumstances have you seen God redeem?

How can you remind yourself of the hope of eternity with God this week?

Transformed by the Word

Bees don't quickly consume the nectar they collect. Instead, they slowly digest it, passing it between one another to further break it down, then carefully storing it in the hive, where the nectar must continue to distill down for much longer before it finally becomes honey.

Sometimes we come to the Bible with a snack mentality—looking for a quick treat—when God's Word is meant to be a lifelong satisfying feast for the soul. This week's study invites you to chew on God's Word like it's the best meal you've ever eaten in your life, digesting its big ideas and experiencing the growth it brings. So feast on the unfathomable riches of God's promises woven throughout the entire Bible. Digest who God is and what he has done for you. Delight in your Savior as you read the Word, study it, and savor it.

God is faithful to reveal eternal truths when we come to digest the big ideas of his Word. As we see God and experience the truth that God sees us and wants to be in relationship with us, we are moved to respond. Whether we respond in belief, action, repentance, worship, or prayer, God's Word is shaping us into a people who reflect his glory to the world. It's in the quiet moments spent with God in his Word that we grow in relationship with him, taste his goodness, and are transformed to be more like our Savior.

Day One | Cross-References

This week will focus on moving from understanding what the text says to understanding what the text means. At this stage, the patterns and themes and main points of the passage start to emerge. You're likely already drawing conclusions about the big ideas of Ephesians 1:1–14 as you've accumulated a lot of knowledge over the past two weeks, but keep holding those ideas loosely. Cross-references will help you check the interpretation beginning to form in your mind, examining it against other parts of Scripture to see if the idea still holds.

I (Maggie) have a hand-painted rendition of Starry Night hanging in my house. I'm no art scholar—I never even took an art composition or history class in college—and I'm definitely not an artist. So the painting hanging in my house almost feels like having the real thing by Van Gogh. Since I've never studied it, I can't really tell you what the differences are and what elements mine might be missing. But if I had the original—not a print, but the real thing—and held them up together, mine would clearly be insufficient.

Cross-references are related verses in the Bible that help you both test the validity of the ideas you're forming and bring clarity to anything you're not sure about. Many (but not all) Bibles include cross-references right within the text. They're the tiny letters in superscript above certain words, and each page will have cross-reference notes in the margin. Open your Bible and look for the cross-references. If your Bible doesn't have them, biblegateway.com has the option to display cross-references in the text.

 Pray for humility and insight before you study God's Word.

GATHER KNOWLEDGE

Read Ephesians 1:1–14. Write down questions that are still unanswered, phrases you're still uncertain about the meaning of, or verses that feel particularly hard to understand.

DIGEST THE BIG IDEAS

Choose one of the questions or challenging concepts you just identified and write the corresponding verse reference(s) in the left column of the chart. Using your own Bible or biblegateway.com, identify three to five related cross-references and write them in the middle column. Then fill in the connection you see between the passage and the cross-reference.

EPHESIANS VERSE(S)	CROSS-REFERENCE	CONNECTION BETWEEN EPHESIANS VERSE(S) AND CROSS-REFERENCE

How do these cross-references bring clarity to the issue(s) you identified in the Gather Knowledge section today?

What did you learn about God, Jesus Christ, or the gospel from today's study?

GROW IN GODLINESS

Circle the way you will respond to God's Word today.

Today I will...   believe   act   repent   worship   pray

Use this space for your response or to plan how you will respond throughout your day.

Write the verse, attribute of God, or gospel truth you will meditate on today.

Day Two | Digest the Main Idea

We live in a digital age. Even much of our social lives have become digital through social media. And social media breeds pride—both a focus on ourselves and a tendency to make quick judgments or jump to conclusions after a shallow consumption of information. Yes, the algorithms and stimulation of the reward center of the human brain exacerbate the issue, but they can't create a problem that wasn't already there.

Bees don't have this issue. Their whole lives are built not around themselves but around the good of the hive. They work hard to play their roles in the greater honey-making process. When we get to the digestion stage of Bible study, we must fight that prideful tendency to center it around ourselves or jump to conclusions or make quick judgments. We need to understand what the text meant to the original audience before we can understand what it means to us.

Digesting the main idea is part of the vital process of turning nectar into honey. Without aiming to understand the main idea for the text's original audience, we risk letting all of our gathering work go to waste because, without the digestion process, it won't become sweet honey to our souls.

Questions to Identify the Main Idea
- What is the author talking about?
- What is the author saying about it?[19]

Questions to Identify the Main Idea in a Narrative Passage
- What is the story about?
- What is the purpose or principle of the story?[20]

After considering these questions, combine your two answers into one sentence. That's your main idea. You might have noticed that, depending on the details you focused on when you gathered knowledge, your main idea could be different from someone else's. That's okay—there's rarely one right way to interpret a complicated passage of Scripture. If you want to check your main idea, ask yourself if you can write three supporting arguments from the text for that main idea.

If you're the woman who feels anxious or unqualified to complete this step, remember this:
- **You've done the work.** You didn't skip the hard stuff and just assume you knew what this passage was saying. You followed the essential principles of Bible study to arrive at this conclusion.
- **You aren't on your own.** The Holy Spirit helps believers understand the Word of God (John 14:26; 16:13).
- **You can clarify and deepen your interpretations through fellowship.** God's Word isn't meant to be studied in isolation. Whenever you can, study God's Word with at least one other person so you can discuss what you're learning and sharpen your interpretations as you discern God's Word together.

- **You can check your interpretations against reliable sources.** After you've studied God's Word for yourself, it's beneficial to check your conclusions against academic sources, like study Bible notes and commentaries. Just be careful not to choose one Bible teacher or scholar and only look to their interpretations. Many teachers from the same theological backgrounds disagree on the meaning of complicated passages.
- **There is always room for correction.** You know who has interpreted the main idea of a passage incorrectly before? Us. And your favorite Bible teacher. And your pastor. And that famous theologian. And the Pharisees. We're going to go out on a limb and say—every person who has ever tried, except Jesus

It's okay if your interpretation isn't perfect or doesn't go as deep as another person's. We're all imperfect so sometimes we're insufficient interpreters of the Bible, but—praise God!—we have a heavenly Father who is well aware that in our human limitations, we won't always get things right. So the next time you realize that you came to the wrong conclusion as you studied God's Word, confess your limitations and rely on the grace offered by your all-powerful God.

 Pray for humility and insight before you study God's Word.

GATHER KNOWLEDGE

Read Ephesians 1:1–14. Look back at all the knowledge you gathered about this passage in Week Two, Week Three Day Five, and yesterday's study. Note anything you think is important to remember about the passage's historical, literary, and redemption story contexts and any other important observations you made.

Historical context

Literary context

Redemption story context

General observations

DIGEST THE BIG IDEAS

What is Paul talking about in Ephesians 1:1–14?

What is Paul saying about it?

What is the main idea of this passage? (Remember: combine your two answers above into one sentence and you have your main idea.)*

What supporting evidence can you offer?

*This is the first time we're not going to offer you an example. Trust the process and ask the Holy Spirit to guide you.

GROW IN GODLINESS

Circle the way you will respond to God's Word today.

Today I will...   believe   act   repent   worship   pray

Use this space for your response or to plan how you will respond throughout your day.

Write the verse, attribute of God, or gospel truth you will meditate on today.

Day Three | Seeing God's Character in All of Scripture

We are constantly changing, but God isn't. He doesn't shift when the world does. He doesn't change his mind or redefine his priorities or purposes. God always stays the same, and the only way to really know him is through his unchanging Word.

The Bible is not a story about us—it's a story about God, and that's exactly what we need. We think we just need to know ourselves and be true to our hearts, but we benefit most from knowing God because his truth is unchanging and his salvation changes us. Ultimately, we enjoy spending time in God's Word because it means we are spending time with God.

Revelation 4:11 describes our infinite and matchless God: "Worthy are you, our Lord and God, to receive glory and honor and power, for you created all things, and by your will they existed and were created." None can be compared to our God, for he is above all things, and he is worthy of all our praise. As we grow in our knowledge of the glorious, awesome, and holy God of the universe, we grow to love him more, we want to obey him more, and we experience the joy of his presence.

Seeing God's character on the pages of the Bible, across chapters and books, and in the overarching redemption story begins with knowing what to look for. Below is a chart of some of God's attributes, their simple definitions, and related verse references. Read through each attribute and its definition.

CREATOR	God created the universe and made humans in his own image.	Gen. 1:1, 26–27; Ps. 102:25; Col. 1:15–16
ETERNAL	God has no beginning and no end. He always has been and always will be.	Isa. 40:28; Hab. 1:12; John 1:1; 1 Tim. 1:17; Rev. 22:13
FAITHFUL	God always keeps his promises.	Deut. 7:9; Ps. 33:4; 2 Thess. 3:3; 2 Tim. 2:13; 1 John 1:9
GOOD	God is kind and always does what is best.	1 Chron. 16:34; Ps. 25:8; 34:8; 136:1; 145:9; Nah. 1:7; Matt. 7:11; Mark 10:18
HOLY	God is set apart and without sin. There is none like him.	Ex. 15:11; Lev. 19:2; 20:26; 1 Sam 2:2; Isa. 6:3; 1 Pet. 1:15

JEALOUS	God deserves all glory and it is always best for us to worship him.	Ex. 20:5; 34:14; Deut. 4:24; 6:15; Josh. 24:19; Nah. 1:2
JUST	God must always judge sin and he always judges in righteousness.	Deut. 32:4; Job 34:12; Ps. 9:7–8; 89:14; Isa. 61:8
LONG-SUFFERING	God is patient and slow to anger, not willing that any should perish but that all would reach repentance.	Ex. 34:6; Num. 14:18; Ps. 86:15; 2 Pet. 3:9
LOVING	God willingly sacrificed himself so we might be saved. His love isn't dependent on our actions and can't be earned. He cares for the needs of his children.	Ps. 136:26; John 3:16; 13:34; 15:13; Rom. 5:8; Eph. 5:25; 1 John 4:7–8, 16, 19
OMNIPOTENT	God is all-powerful. He isn't impacted by the physical laws of the universe.	Job 42:2; Ps. 147:5; Jer. 32:17; Matt. 19:26; Rom. 1:20
OMNIPRESENT	God is always present, everywhere, at all times. He exists outside of time.	Deut. 31:8; Ps. 139:7–10; Prov. 15:3; Jer. 23:24
OMNISCIENT	God knows all things, including our thoughts and the deepest desires of our hearts.	Ps. 147:5; Prov. 15:3; Isa. 40:28; Rom. 11:33–36; 1 John 3:20
RIGHTEOUS	God is always right and pure. What's right and wrong is based on his character and his law.	Ps. 11:7; Rom. 3:21; 10:3–4; 1 John 2:1
SOVEREIGN	God is in charge. He rules the universe and our lives. Nothing happens outside of his will.	Prov. 16:33; Matt. 10:29–31; Rom. 8:28; Eph. 1:4
UNCHANGING	God's nature, will, and promises are the same yesterday, today, and forever.	Isa. 40:8; Mal. 3:6; Heb. 13:8; James 1:17
WISE	God always knows what is best.	Job 12:13; Prov. 3:19; Isa. 55:9; Rom. 16:27

Pray for humility and insight before you study God's Word.

GATHER KNOWLEDGE

Read Ephesians 1:1–14. List God's actions in this passage.

Review the list of God's attributes and write down any you see in this passage.

DIGEST THE BIG IDEAS

What did you learn about God from today's study?

GROW IN GODLINESS

Circle the way you will respond to God's Word today.

Today I will...   believe   act   repent   worship   pray

Use this space for your response or to plan how you will respond throughout your day.

Write the verse, attribute of God, or gospel truth you will meditate on today.

Day Four | Seeing Jesus Christ in All of Scripture

One day, I (Gretchen) wake up before dawn and start the day soaking in the Word while sipping my coffee. The next, I press snooze and get to the end of the day without cracking open my Bible.

One day, I hear alarming news and still praise God and trust him with what's to come. The next, I find myself questioning him and worrying about tomorrow.

One day, Christ is first in my heart and everything else falls into place. The next, I put him second—the dominos start to fall, and I don't go to him for help.

The difference between these contrasting days is what I put first, or shall I say, who I put first. C.S. Lewis explains, "You can't get second things by putting them first; you can get second things only by putting first things first."[21] If we want to have abundant lives on earth, we won't get them by seeking the things of this world. Second things can only be enjoyed by putting Christ first. When spending time with Jesus is the first priority in our lives, the second things fall into place.

The primary way we seek to know, love, and put Jesus first in our lives is through Bible study. Jesus isn't just the main character of the Gospels; he's the main character of all of Scripture. The Old Testament is filled with humanity's desperate need for a Savior. It also includes prophecies and promises that point to Jesus as the coming Rescuer, the solution for all of humanity's sin. The Old Testament stories also sometimes feature people who demonstrate aspects of the coming Savior while gently whispering that he will be even better.

The New Testament reveals Jesus Christ as the promised Savior. The Gospels show how Jesus is the promised Messiah. They contain Jesus' very words to people desperately in need of him and his loving actions to lead them to repentance. The rest of the New Testament tells of the foundation of the church and explains how Jesus' life, death, and resurrection transform our lives. The New Testament also offers the hope of Jesus' future return and the glories of eternity with God in the new heaven and new earth. When we seek to know Jesus through all the pages of God's Word, our hearts will be transformed and we will put him first.

Questions to See Jesus Christ in the Old Testament
- How does this passage show humanity's need for Jesus?
- What prophecies or promises in this passage show that Jesus is coming?
- What good things or people in this passage show glimpses of who Jesus will be? How will Jesus Christ be even better?

Questions to See Jesus Christ in the Gospels
- What does Jesus say or do in this passage?

- What do Jesus' actions in this passage display about his character?
- What do Jesus' actions in this passage display about his purposes?

Questions to See Jesus Christ in the New Testament
- What does this passage explicitly say about Jesus?
- How does this passage utilize a principle, teaching, or event from the life of Jesus?
- How does this passage show Jesus' impact on a believer's past, present, or future?

 Pray for humility and insight before you study God's Word.

GATHER KNOWLEDGE

Read Ephesians 1:1–14. What does this passage explicitly say about Jesus?

DIGEST THE BIG IDEAS

How does this passage utilize a principle, teaching, or event from the life of Jesus?

How does this passage show Jesus' impact on a believer's past, present, or future?

What did you learn about Jesus Christ from today's study?

GROW IN GODLINESS

Circle the way you will respond to God's Word today.

Today I will...   believe   act   repent   worship   pray

Use this space for your response or to plan how you will respond throughout your day.

Write the verse, attribute of God, or gospel truth you will meditate on today.

Day Five | Grow in Godliness

I (Maggie) have been asking my friends about their earliest memories of honey, and I'm surprised that almost everyone has one. Mine is of a friend whose peanut butter and honey sandwiches were so much tastier than mine. Around thirty years later, I realized her mom was using raw honey smeared thick on organic bread—there's just no comparison to the good stuff. Around the same time I had this revelation, my husband introduced me to his first memory of honey: buying the whole honeycomb, sucking the honey out, and chewing on the comb. Honey is special—it sticks with you, on your fingers, in your mind, in your soul.

And for the bee, honey isn't just something to drizzle on a warm buttery biscuit fresh from the oven—honey is their sustenance. If you are a believer, God's Word both sustains you in whatever circumstances you're facing and helps you grow in godliness. This third principle of Bible study is absolutely essential to maturing as a Christian. The Holy Spirit uses God's Word to grow your faith, grow you to be more like Christ, and grow abundant spiritual fruit in your life.

So when you've done the work of gathering knowledge about God's Word and digesting the big ideas, don't keep what you've learned up in your head. Let it seep down into your heart to transform your desires and motives and, ultimately, your actions. What you learned about God through his Word should be sticky—getting all over whatever you touch. And once you've digested the big ideas, they should change you, shaping your character and causing spiritual growth. Remember, you are what you eat.

Hearty application involves considering how the big ideas you've digested impact how you interact with God and the world and people around you. The main idea of the passage should impact your life and your particular set of circumstances. Set aside time every day to respond to God by choosing to believe a truth from his Word over a lie of the world, taking specific action in your current circumstances, worshiping God for who he is, repenting of your sin, or praying for your own heart. Since we are forgetful creatures, identify a truth from God's Word to continue to meditate on throughout the day, considering how it impacts any big or small decisions you make or hardships you face.

Questions to Grow in Godliness
- How might the main idea of the passage apply to your circumstances?
- How will you respond?
- What will you remember?

Good application of God's Word to our lives is hard. It's easier to keep it in our heads than let it impact our hearts. It's easier to recognize how someone else should feel convicted by its message than to respond with repentance. So do the hard work of heart work. Get honest before God and pray, asking him how he wants the truths you uncovered in his Word to impact your life. Bring your insufficiencies and failures, your insecurities and doubts, your questions and concerns before the lamp of God's Word and experience insight and freedom for your everyday life.

Pray for humility and insight before you study God's Word.

GATHER KNOWLEDGE

Read Ephesians 1:1–14 for the final time in this study, preparing your heart to make final applications from this passage.

DIGEST THE BIG IDEAS

Review your answers from each day of study this week. Ask the Holy Spirit to reveal how what you learned from God's Word impacts your life.

GROW IN GODLINESS

How might the main idea of Ephesians 1:1–14 apply to your circumstances?

Circle the way you will respond to God's Word today.

Today I will...   believe   act   repent   worship   pray

Use this space for your response or to plan how you will respond throughout your day.

Write the verse, attribute of God, or gospel truth you will meditate on today.

Session Four Viewer Guide

_____

_____

_____

_____

_____

_____

_____

_____

_____

_____

_____

_____

_____

_____

_____

_____

_____

_____

_____

_____

_____

_____

_____

QUESTIONS FOR DISCUSSION OR REFLECTION

Consider these responses to God's Word: believe, act, repent, worship, pray. Which responses come easily to you?

Which response do you want to grow in? Commit to responding in this way in the Grow in Godliness section of your Bible study at least twice this week.

The Word in Every Season

While honey is a delight to many, young and old, it's essentially poison to a baby. Their immature digestive systems don't have the resources to process it until they're older. Similarly, through spiritual maturity, we develop the resources necessary to process God's Word well. In the twelfth century, Jewish people in Germany created a custom around taking children to school for the first time. A rabbi ceremonially placed honey on slates made for learning and the brave children would lick it. The children would also eat honey cakes inscribed with verses about God's Word.[22] These outward ceremonies demonstrated that tasting the sweetness of God's Word is for those ready and willing to learn, who are growing in maturity. As you mature in your faith, you don't need less of God's Word but more, and as you grow in your dependence on God, his Word becomes sweeter than honey.

Learning to study God's Word is a lifelong process. We hope you feel equipped with the principles you need to study well by the time you complete this study, but you don't have to know how to do everything perfectly. As you grow in your ability to study God's Word, you'll grow in spiritual maturity, and that maturity will also fuel your ability to understand God's Word. Over time, you'll see that the disciplines you've developed in this study have grown into delight in God's Word.

This week explains different methods of Bible study that utilize the gather, digest, and grow principles. Each method serves a different purpose, develops different kinds of Bible knowledge, and fits with different kinds of seasons. There will likely be one Bible study method you prefer from this week, but take time to consider the benefits of each one. Then, when seasons turn and change inevitably comes, you'll know how to keep your feet firmly planted on God's unchangeable Word.

Day One | Study the Bible from Start to Finish

Reading the Bible from start to finish is a common method of Bible study, but it's definitely not easy. While Bible reading plans often encourage us to complete this task in a year, that's not always a reasonable pace for many women depending on their season. Rather, this same approach can easily be stretched into two to five years. However long it takes, the benefits include reading portions of the Bible you'd normally skip (hello, Leviticus and Job), seeing the redemption story of God's Word from Genesis to Revelation, discovering the connecting themes that run through Scripture, and better understanding how the New Testament comes from the context of the Old Testament.

When I (Gretchen) read through the Bible in a year for the first time, I took great pride in what I accomplished. I began the marathon, so to speak, and I finished it—goal complete. I decided to start again the next year, but life's challenges reared against me and I quickly fell behind. My perfectionism screamed at me, and the growing number of unchecked boxes kept me from continuing. I thought, *Who wants to run a race in last place?* So I quit.

Sometimes the motivation for reading our Bibles becomes completion rather than developing an intimate relationship with God. But the goal of Bible study isn't to puff up one's soul or place a big check mark at the end of the year. The goal is to know God more through his Word, to come hungry and humbled before him, and to glorify him in our reading, worship, and obedience.

Don't let the potential pitfalls of pride or perfection stop you from pursuing the discipline of daily Bible study! Let your Bible reading be led by grace, not guilt. The goal isn't to build your good Christian resume; the goal is to know and love God more.

When you study the Bible from start to finish, the large amount of chapters you read each day will necessitate simpler study. This method is about breadth, not depth. But that doesn't mean you don't work to gather knowledge before digesting big ideas. Instead, focus much of your daily study on summarizing what you read each day. Then, identify the big ideas not simply from that day's study alone but from how that passage fits within the larger context of what you've already read in the Bible. For example, you might choose to pay specific attention to the patterns of the redemption story you read in each passage, and over time, you'll begin to see the bigger patterns emerging even more clearly.

This method is wonderful for understanding the Bible as one big story, but it doesn't allow for you to dig deeply into the specific meaning of each passage you read. Reading the entire Bible from start to finish is definitely time-consuming, so be reasonable when setting your goal for how soon you can complete it and recognize when the limitations of your current season might require you to go at a pace that will take multiple years to finish.

Pray for humility and insight before you study God's Word.

GATHER KNOWLEDGE

Over the next two days, you'll read all of the book of Ruth. Don't worry—it's just four chapters. If you have the time, consider reading or listening to the entire book of Ruth both today and tomorrow. Remember, if you were reading the book of Ruth within the context of reading the entire Bible from start to finish, you wouldn't have time to slow down and interpret every verse. Instead, pay attention to big ideas, themes, and the redemption story as a whole. Today you'll consider context and genre questions.

What genre is the book of Ruth? Refer back to Week Two Day Three and review the brief notes, questions, and literary styles to consider when studying this type of book.

Read Ruth 1–2. When do the events recorded in Ruth take place (v. 1)?

Where does Elimelech move his family? Why?

Who is in the story? What are their relationships to each other? Consider answering with a visual representation of their relationships.

What painful experiences does Naomi face in Moab?

Read Ruth 1:13, 19–21 again. How does Naomi describe herself? Why?

Read Ruth 1:15–18 again and summarize Ruth's response to Naomi in one sentence.

Review Ruth 2 and write a one or two-sentence summary of each passage.

Ruth 2:1–7

Ruth 2:8–13

Ruth 2:14–17

Ruth 2:18–23

DIGEST THE BIG IDEAS

How does Ruth show kindness to Naomi?

How does Boaz show kindness to Ruth?

Look again at Ruth 2:19–21. Do you agree with Naomi's assessment of God's actions toward her in verse 20? Why or why not?

What does this story display about God's relationship with his covenant people?

What did you learn about God, Jesus Christ, or the gospel from today's study?

GROW IN GODLINESS

Circle the way you will respond to God's Word today.

Today I will...   believe   act   repent   worship   pray

Use this space for your response or to plan how you will respond throughout your day.

Write the verse, attribute of God, or gospel truth you will meditate on today.

Day Two | Study the Bible by Theme

If you pay attention to enough stories, you'll soon recognize that most of them are based on the oldest and best story of all. They show that the world is broken, people aren't doing well, and they desperately need something or someone to fix their circumstances or save them. In the end, the hero defeats the villain and all is right in the world, and everyone lives happily ever after.

This storyline captures our attention over and over again because this is the story that we are living in. The whole world is broken, and something within us tells us it's not supposed to be this way. There's only one seemingly impossible solution, but this requires more than an imperfect hero—it requires a perfect Savior. This is God's redemption story, and it's our story too when we put our faith in Jesus Christ.

Understanding the Bible as one story and recognizing how the pieces fit together is called *biblical theology*. The backbone of biblical theology is the redemption story that you studied in Week Three. Studying the Bible by theme starts with identifying where a passage falls on the timeline of redemptive history and which patterns of creation, fall, redemption, and consummation are evident. But you can take it a step deeper by looking for the literary symbols and themes that God sprinkled throughout the redemption story. Good literature uses themes and symbols to demonstrate something true about the human experience or the world we're living in. And no work of literature does this as well as the Bible—God is the best Author, after all.

This type of study uses the same principles of gather, digest, and grow, but the digestion stage focuses on a specific theme or literary symbol evident in the text. We recommend starting with a specific book of the Bible and using the introduction in a study Bible to identify key themes of that book that you want to pay attention to. Once you've gotten comfortable recognizing the themes within a book, you'll be more confident in identifying themes across books and across the entire redemption story, and you'll see how they develop through the stages of creation, fall, redemption, and consummation.

Example Themes to Study: land, offspring/child, tree, water, wilderness, dwelling (including the tabernacle and temple), kingdom, covenant, mediator (pay attention to the roles of prophet, priest, and king), sacrifice, rest, clothing, wedding/marriage

Pray for humility and insight before you study God's Word.

GATHER KNOWLEDGE

Today's study will consider the book of Ruth in light of the Bible's redemption story, including the theme of redemption that dominates Ruth 3–4. Remember to read or listen to the entire book today if you're able.

During which period of redemptive history does the book of Ruth take place? What are some of the important elements of living in that part of the story? Review Week Three Day Three if you need help.

Read Ruth 2:20. This is the first mention of a redeemer in the book of Ruth. Who does it refer to?

Look up a definition for the word *redeem*.

Read Ruth 3–4. Note how many times you see these words: *bought, redeem, redeemer,* and *redemption*.

Summarize the events of each chapter in four or five sentences or bullet points. Note that when summarizing an entire chapter of historical narrative, you'll only be able to include major events, not details.

Ruth 3

Ruth 4

DIGEST THE BIG IDEAS

Choose one of these questions to answer about the pattern of creation displayed in the book of Ruth.

- How is God's rule and authority as sovereign Creator evident?
- How are people fulfilling or abdicating their roles as cultivators and caretakers of creation?
- How are people bearing the image of God or not?

Choose one of these questions to answer about the pattern of the fall displayed in the book of Ruth.

- How is humanity's sinfulness or rebellion against God's rule evident?
- Are there any elements of the brokenness of creation?
- How is God's judgment handled in this passage?

Choose one of these questions to answer about the pattern of redemption displayed in the book of Ruth.

- Who needs rescue? Who is providing rescue?
- Are there any promises made or needs highlighted that can only be fulfilled or resolved by a Savior?
- Are the people this text is written to living under the old or new covenant? How does that impact their relationship with God?

Choose one of these questions to answer about the pattern of consummation displayed in the book of Ruth.

- How is God currently dwelling with his people?
- Are the people of God at home? Why or why not?
- What are God's people placing their hope in?
- Are there any promises that won't be fulfilled until Christ comes again?

What did you learn about God, Jesus Christ, or the gospel from today's study?

GROW IN GODLINESS

Circle the way you will respond to God's Word today.

Today I will...   believe   act   repent   worship   pray

Use this space for your response or to plan how you will respond throughout your day.

Write the verse, attribute of God, or gospel truth you will meditate on today.

Day Three | Study the Bible Verse by Verse

The most straightforward method for studying God's Word is to choose a book of the Bible and go through it slowly, verse by verse. Read a small portion of Scripture and study it until you're confident in the big ideas you've digested, then move on to the next portion. This method is the jeans and white tee of Bible study—it can be adapted to fit almost any season or circumstance, and you should come back to it over and over. It's the method you used to study Ephesians 1:1–14. When you close this study and wonder what you're going to do next, we'd encourage you to keep going through Ephesians. It's a rich book that's absolutely essential to spiritual maturity.

Reading the Bible verse by verse works in so many seasons because you don't have to finish it all in one day. You can sit in each principle of study—gather, digest, and grow—for however long you need to study a short passage, then move on to the next one. So whether you have five minutes a day or forty-five minutes a day, you can study a book of the Bible verse by verse.

 Pray for humility and insight before you study God's Word.

GATHER KNOWLEDGE

Read Ruth 4:13–17. Today's study will dig into this short passage verse by verse.

Look at verse 13. What happens? Who is in control of it?

Look at verse 14. Who is rejoicing with Naomi?

Who gets the praise for sending the redeemer for Naomi?

Look at verse 15. What will the redeemer be to Naomi?

The number seven is a symbol for completion or fullness. So what value does Ruth have in Naomi's life?

Look at verse 16. What kind of relationship does Naomi have with Ruth and Boaz's child?

Look at verse 17. What is Obed's relationship to David?

Describe Naomi at the beginning of the book of Ruth. Look back at Ruth 1:19–21 if necessary.

Describe Naomi at the end of the book of Ruth.

DIGEST THE BIG IDEAS

What does the change in Naomi demonstrate about redemption?

Why is Obed's relationship to David significant? What better redemption is this verse hinting at?

What kind of honor does this bestow on Naomi?

Read Matthew 1:1, 5–6. What place of honor does God give to Ruth and Boaz?

Consider what you've learned about the book of Ruth this week. What is the story of the book of Ruth about?

What is the purpose or principle of the story?

Now look back at Ruth 4:13–17. Considering the larger context of the book of Ruth that you just identified, what is the main idea of this passage?

What attributes of God are displayed in Ruth 4:13–17?

How does the book of Ruth show humanity's need for Jesus?

What people in this story show us a glimpse of who Jesus will be? How will Jesus Christ be even better?

GROW IN GODLINESS

How might the main idea of Ruth 4:13–17 apply to your circumstances?

Circle the way you will respond to God's Word today.

Today I will...   believe   act   repent   worship   pray

Use this space for your response or to plan how you will respond throughout your day.

Write the verse, attribute of God, or gospel truth you will meditate on today.

Day Four | Study the Bible by Topic

Have you ever tried to explain the Trinity to a child? Or tried to explain the concept of sin to someone who doesn't know Christ? Or maybe in the middle of studying your Bible or in the middle of your everyday life, you suddenly realize that you've read or used words like *grace* or *redemption* or *sanctification*, but you can't really explain what they mean. Maybe when you try to define terms, you find yourself relying on old sayings you learned in church as a child, but you don't really know if Scripture supports them. Let's face it—Christianity is complex. But instead of just walking through life with a vague sense of the meaning of theological terms or just choosing a favorite Bible teacher and adopting whatever definition they give you for a theological term, you can study God's Word to define terms for yourself.

Topical study can get a bad rap in the church, but that's because in our pride, we tend to choose topics that are all about us and then take verses out of context to fit the meaning we need for our current circumstances. But when we open the Bible seeking to know something about God or the gospel and understand its definition across all of Scripture, we are actually doing systematic theology. As you mature in your faith, you want to develop both a *biblical theology* (an understanding of the redemption story of the Bible and how its themes are revealed over time) and a *systematic theology* (an understanding of what the entire Bible has to say about a specific topic).

I (Maggie) tend to incorporate topical study when I'm already studying a passage and come across a theological term that I can't define for myself, when I feel stuck in a sin pattern, when I'm struggling to believe what I know to be true about God's character or the gospel, or when I just need wisdom about a specific topic. I start by reading every reference included in a Bible dictionary definition or by using the search feature on biblegateway.com to see how the word is used across all of Scripture. As I take notes, I notice repeated ideas. I also pay attention to genre and literary style, where the passage falls in the Bible's redemption story, and the context of the passage. If two verses seem to be opposed to each other, further study of those passages in their context is necessary.

Once I've reviewed all the passages I can find, I attempt to write a definition of the term myself, using language specifically lifted from the verses I've studied. Finally, I check my conclusion against a few biblical scholars. If this kind of study sounds like a lot of work, that's because it is. But it's also easily split across multiple days (or weeks, depending on the size of the topic!), so its flexibility works well with busy schedules. This kind of study works best as part of a broader study of a book of the Bible. It's a way to deepen your knowledge and understanding of that book while developing your systematic theology.

Pray for humility and insight before you study God's Word.

GATHER KNOWLEDGE

Today you'll consider what the New Testament has to say about redemption. Read the following verses and take notes on how redemption is described.

Romans 3:23–24

Romans 8:22–23

1 Corinthians 1:30

Galatians 4:4–5

Ephesians 1:7

Ephesians 4:30

Colossians 1:13–14

Titus 2:13–14

Hebrews 9:12

Put a star next to the verse references that refer to still awaiting the consummation of our redemption.

What themes or details are repeated across all these verses?

DIGEST THE BIG IDEAS

What is different from the redemption that happens in the book of Ruth and the redemption described in the New Testament verses you read today?

How would you explain or define New Testament redemption according to the verses you read today?

What did you learn about God, Jesus Christ, or the gospel from today's study?

GROW IN GODLINESS

Circle the way you will respond to God's Word today.

Today I will...   believe   act   repent   worship   pray

Use this space for your response or to plan how you will respond throughout your day.

Write the verse, attribute of God, or gospel truth you will meditate on today.

Day Five | Stay in the Bible in Hard Seasons

When I (Maggie) gave birth to my second son, I went through one of the longest periods of not being in the Word I had ever experienced. For the first time in my life, Bible study just couldn't look like sitting down with God's Word for thirty uninterrupted minutes. My first son had napped in my arms as I read my Bible every morning, but with two little ones, nap schedules didn't align and I was so incredibly exhausted. I felt like there was no point in reading my Bible since I couldn't do it the "right" way. So I quit. I didn't even realize I had given up until I was months into a life without God's Word. But life without God's Word is lifeless. The temptation to quit is always there, lurking, and it's exactly what the enemy would have us do—because quitting on the Bible means a stagnant relationship with God.

So make a plan now for how you'll get in God's Word in hard seasons so that you don't give up the next time you experience one. Even in seasons when we're exhausted or suffering or distracted or grieving or doubting or our brains just feel like mush, we can still study God's Word the same way we always do—with the help of the Holy Spirit. And on the days when opening your Bible feels impossible or overwhelming, try one of these two methods.

Start with the Psalms. Just read (or even listen to) one psalm every day. This may be all you have the time or mental capacity to do. That's okay. Remember that being in God's Word is about developing a relationship with God, not earning your salvation or proving your worth. If you're able, try to apply the gather, digest, and grow principles to what you're reading. Let the emotions and prayers of the psalmist touch your heart, but don't miss who God is and the glimpses of Jesus woven throughout. As your season settles down or your heart heals, go back to deeper study of God's Word.

Read verse by verse very slowly. Set aside five minutes a day and read five verses or less.[23] Give yourself one to five days to complete each principle—gathering, digesting, and growing slowly. This slow plodding of faithfulness will bear fruit over time as you commit to putting Jesus first, even in really challenging seasons.

Remember: the God who created space and time has ordained this hard season in your life to grow your dependence on him. So keep pursuing your relationship with God through his Word. When your circumstances taste bitter, may the message of redemption that permeates the Bible be sweet like honey to your soul. When you don't know what God is doing, rest in his presence, knowing that he can redeem your circumstances for your good and his glory.

Pray for humility and insight before you study God's Word.

GATHER KNOWLEDGE

Read Psalm 103 and mark any verses or words that remind you of God's redemption story.

Write Psalm 103:2–5 below.

DIGEST THE BIG IDEAS

What connections do you see between the themes of this psalm and the themes of the book of Ruth?

What attributes of God do you see displayed in Psalm 103?

What glimpses of Jesus or the gospel do you see in Psalm 103?

GROW IN GODLINESS

Which verses from Psalm 103 did your soul need today?

Circle the way you will respond to God's Word today.

Today I will...   believe   act   repent   worship   pray

Use this space for your response or to plan how you will respond throughout your day.

Write the verse, attribute of God, or gospel truth you will meditate on today.

Session Five Viewer Guide

_____

_____

_____

_____

_____

_____

_____

_____

_____

_____

_____

_____

_____

_____

_____

_____

_____

_____

_____

_____

QUESTIONS FOR DISCUSSION OR REFLECTION

What benefits of fellowship in God's Word have you experienced?

What keeps you from talking about God's Word with other people?

What relationship would benefit from you bravely sharing what God has taught you in his Word recently?

The Word in Everyday Life

Nectar gives bees a natural sugar rush, so they always want to gather more. But some flowers play a tricky game—they mix in small amounts of caffeine or nicotine with their nectar, so the bees are more quickly satisfied, collecting less nectar on each visit. But those substances are even more addictive than a sugar rush, so the bees go back to the same insufficient flowers again and again, never satisfied. The flowers get more pollination while offering less to the bees.

What things in your life do you go to again and again but never truly satisfy you? What does your mind remain fixated on even when your body gets busy with the work of your daily life? My (Maggie's) mind often remains stuck in whatever content I've been consuming online or whatever dangerously addictive app I've been foolish enough to download onto my phone. So while I may be actively doing the work God has given me, my mind continues to search for satisfaction in the escapes of the world.

Despite the fake satisfaction that a flower may offer a bee, bees are good at remaining fixated on the source of their lives: their hive. It's not that they never leave the hive but that they keep returning to it over and over that makes the difference. When they return to the hive, the nectar they collected turns into the fruit of honey.

God's Word is the source of our life—it's where we receive the nourishment of a relationship with God, the honey that truly satisfies. So Jesus told his disciples in John 15:5, "I am the vine; you are the branches. Whoever abides in me and I in him, he it is that bears much fruit, for apart from me you can do nothing." To abide is simply to remain. So if we remain in Christ, not just opening our Bibles in the morning but sticking near him in relationship all day, we will bear fruit.

So far this study has been focused on the study of God's Word, but it doesn't matter how deeply we've studied God's Word if we close our Bibles and forget that God exists for the rest of the day. This is one of the most common and most important battles of the Christian life—not just knowing about God and the truth of his Word but living it, remembering it in the mundane and the chaotic moments, depending on it throughout our days. So we build habits that help us remain near to God in our daily lives. I (Maggie) like to attach these spiritual disciplines to specific habits that already exist in my day, creating rhythms of remaining with God. This week will consider spiritual disciplines that help you both deepen your study of God's Word and incorporate it into the habits of your everyday life.

Day One | Linger in the Word

I (Maggie) finally gave in to my husband's desire to keep bees, so as I write this, we're about to get our first two hives. By the time you're actually reading this, our bees will—Lord willing—be surviving their first Minnesota winter. As beekeepers, we'll aid the bees in establishing their hives and be careful to avoid harvesting too much honey so they'll have plenty of nourishment to survive even the harshest weather.

When we finish our Bible study and go about our days, we face the winds of the world and hearts that are cold to the gospel, so we must keep near the sweet truth of God's Word. We're prone to think either too harshly or too highly of ourselves and to make either too little or too much of our circumstances. So we need the wisdom of God's Word to help us discern the thoughts and intentions of our own hearts (Heb. 4:12). We need the grace of the gospel when our hearts condemn us (1 John 3:20; Rom. 8:1). We need the comfort of God's promises to give us hope when our minds are prone to despair (Ps. 23:4). When we run to God's Word to meet these needs, it becomes our delight, like honey to our lips.

Psalm 1:1–3 describes a believer who is like a tree that stands strong and prospers in any season. The primary mark of that believer is that "his delight is in the law of the LORD, and on his law he meditates day and night" (Ps. 1:2). Those who stay strong in the harsh weather of everyday life are those who delight in God's Word. But we can't experience the delight of God's Word without lingering. Meditating on God's Word moves you from simply consuming the truth of the Word to seeing the God who wrote the truth, made the promise, remained faithful, sacrificed himself, intercedes for us, and transforms us. Meditation is entering into relationship with God, and that relationship makes his Word sweeter than honey.

Biblical meditation is like the honey bee's regurgitation process of digesting nectar into honey. It's recalling God's Word again and again until it permeates and transforms your soul. There are many different practical methods of biblical meditation, but they all involve slowness and repetition. Theologian Tim Keller suggests asking these questions of the Scripture you're meditating on: *Am I living in light of this? What difference does this make? Am I taking this seriously? If I believed and held to this, how would that change things? When I forget this, how does that affect me and all my relationships?* [24] These questions help you meditate on a text that you've previously studied. They incline your heart to God's Word after your head has already engaged with it.

Another common method is to repeat a verse out loud, emphasizing a different word each time and noting how the emphasis develops your understanding of the meaning of the text. You can also memorize and repeat the verse throughout your day, asking the Holy Spirit to open your eyes to how this verse matters in your everyday life. Consider tying this rhythm of remaining to an everyday habit like eating breakfast, checking your email, or doing the dishes.

Pray for humility and insight before you study God's Word.

GATHER KNOWLEDGE

Read John 15:1–11. What genre is the book of John?

Who is speaking in these verses?

Read John 13:1–4 for the context of these verses. Who is Jesus speaking to? What are the circumstances? What is about to happen?

Return to John 15:1–11. Look up the word *abide* and write your own definition.

Summarize verses 1–6 in two sentences.

Summarize verses 7–11 in two sentences.

What should abide in a believer according to verse 7?

DIGEST THE BIG IDEAS

Why was it important for the disciples to learn about abiding in Christ right before Jesus died on the cross?

What is Jesus talking about in John 15:1–11?

What is he saying about it?

What is the main idea of this passage? (Remember: combine your two answers above into one sentence and you have your main idea.)

Read John 8:31–32. What does abiding in God's Word prove? What impact does it have?

How is biblical meditation a form of abiding in God's Word?

What value does it then have?

What did you learn about God, Jesus Christ, or the gospel from today's study?

GROW IN GODLINESS

How might the main idea of John 15:1–11 apply to your circumstances?

Circle the way you will respond to God's Word today.

Today I will...   believe   act   repent   worship   pray

Use this space for your response or to plan how you will respond throughout your day.

Write the verse, attribute of God, or gospel truth you will meditate on today.

Day Two | Pray the Word

Why is it that when I (Gretchen) open my Bible, my mind immediately wanders? Sometimes the thoughts are incredibly random, like my brain is sorting through a junk drawer of the things I've seen and consumed recently. Other times they're specific to my current struggles, revolving worries about the day and weeks ahead. With the help of the Holy Spirit, we can acknowledge our wild thoughts and turn back to the truths of Scripture. We can process them in the presence of Jesus, unpacking them bit by bit as we pray through them and preach the Word that we're reading to our hearts.

If your mind starts to wander as you read God's Word, or your heart feels numb to God's truth, or your worries make you unable to concentrate, or the passage you're reading feels too challenging to comprehend, pray. Prayer is an essential part of the Bible study process—we can't focus on the Word, understand the Word, or be changed by the Word without humble hearts and the help of the Holy Spirit.

For around fifteen years, I (Maggie) have used a helpful tool called the IOUS of prayer that I first learned from theologian John Piper.[25] I do my best to pray all or some of these verses whenever I study God's Word.

I	<u>Incline</u> my heart to your testimonies, and not to selfish gain! Psalm 119:36	This prayer addresses our desperate need for God to create a desire for his Word in our hearts.
O	<u>Open</u> my eyes, that I may behold wondrous things out of your law. Psalm 119:18	This prayer acknowledges that we can't understand God's Word without his help.
U	<u>Unite</u> my heart to fear your name. Psalm 86:11c	This prayer identifies that our hearts tend to be divided between God and the gifts of this world. It asks God to help us focus our hearts on loving him first and foremost.
S	<u>Satisfy</u> us in the morning with your steadfast love, that we may rejoice and be glad all our days. Psalm 90:14	This prayer reminds our souls that only God provides the joy and satisfaction we're constantly seeking.

And even though adding an L messes up the acronym, I recently read about incorporating this final prayer:

| L | Lead me, O Lord, in your righteousness. Psalm 5:8a | This prayer turns the focus of Bible study from pure academic knowledge to soul transformation and growing in Christlikeness. |

While prayer is an essential part of our study of God's Word, God's Word is also an essential part of our prayer lives. If we want to ask God for things that are within his will, we must know his will as outlined in the Bible. God isn't our spiritual vending machine. Instead, he invites us into his work through prayer. Try setting aside a certain time each day when you will pray specifically using a verse from the passage you're studying or the main idea, attribute of God, or truth about Jesus Christ or the gospel that you digested in that day's study. Tie this specific time of prayer to an everyday habit like brushing your teeth, showering, driving, or eating lunch, and you will have created a rhythm of remaining that keeps you near to God through his Word.

 Pray for humility and insight before you study God's Word. Consider using the IOUS+L acronym to guide your prayer today.

GATHER KNOWLEDGE

Read John 15:1–11. Now look closely at verse 7, the focus of today's study.

> If you abide in me, and my words abide in you, ask whatever you wish, and it will be done for you.
> John 15:7

Circle the word *ask*. It's the primary action of the sentence (or the predicate for you grammar buffs). Now underline and number the two conditions of asking (they come after the word *if*).

Rewrite verse 7 in your own words.

DIGEST THE BIG IDEAS

How does abiding in Christ and his words abiding in us transform the way we ask for something?

How does it transform what we ask for?

Why does abiding in Christ and his words abiding in us make the sweeping promise "it will be done for you" possible?

Read John 14:13–14. What similar promise does Jesus make in these verses?

What is the condition of the asking in these verses?

Do you think this just means including "in Jesus' name" at the end of a prayer? Why or why not?

What is a person's name synonymous with? How does this shed light on what Jesus means by this condition?

Read 1 John 5:14. How are we to pray according to this verse?

Read 1 Thessalonians 5:17. What connection do you see between prayer and abiding in this verse?

How do prayer and studying God's Word work together?

What did you learn about God, Jesus Christ, or the gospel from today's study?

GROW IN GODLINESS

Circle the way you will respond to God's Word today.

Today I will...   believe   act   repent   worship   pray

Use this space for your response or to plan how you will respond throughout your day.

Write the verse, attribute of God, or gospel truth you will meditate on today.

Day Three | Love the Word

The summer before I started tenth grade, my (Maggie's) mom invited me to join the Bible study she was leading for college women. It became one of the most important invitations of my life. That summer, I developed a deep and abiding love for God's Word as I uncovered new layers of meaning and caught the Bible teacher's contagious passion for the Word. The Bible was no longer just the moralistic tales of my childhood—it was an opportunity to learn to live in relationship with my Savior. At the end of the summer, I was desperate for more. I asked my mom to lead a group of my friends through another study. She spent the next eleven years leading a weekly Bible study for high school girls in our home. During the introductory week of each new study, she'd hold up her Bible and offer the same exhortation: *It's good to study the Bible to know what God's Word says, but do you love it? Is it sweeter than honey to you?* I still meet or reconnect with women today who tell me that the Bible study my mom led was the first time they fell in love with God's Word.

In today's culture, God's Word—especially the commands of Scripture—is rarely loved, hardly treasured, and often even met with disdain. It's considered outdated and out of touch and sometimes downright hateful. But our culture has missed the point. God didn't create an arbitrary list of rules to trip us up. His commands demonstrate the path to abundant life. The world tells us to endlessly pursue our desires; God's Word shows us that our desires are satisfied in God alone. The world tells us to make our own truth; the Bible is the inerrant truth that keeps us steadfast in any trial. The world tells us that material things will give us life; God's Word says that Jesus is the way, the truth, and the life. God's way is the best way because it's the only way that leads us to him.

We can't love and value God if we don't spend regular time in his Word to learn about him and build a relationship with him. As Bible teacher Jen Wilkin famously says, "The heart cannot love what the mind does not know."[26] So if you don't feel a deep and abiding love for God and his Word, the answer isn't to avoid the Bible but to spend more time in it. Search the pages of Scripture not for more of yourself but for more of your Savior. See the redemption story God was writing before the foundations of the world. Grasp the riches of God's grace and the boundlessness of God's love for you. Even a glimpse of God's love displayed in the gospel and written throughout all the pages of Scripture can spark a passion to know and love God more through his Word. When you abide in Christ and his words abide in you, you grow to love his Word and obey it and you experience the joy of fruitful life in Christ.

Pray for humility and insight before you study God's Word.

GATHER KNOWLEDGE

Read John 15:1–11. Today's study will focus on verses 8–11. First look at verse 7. What two kinds of abiding serve as the foundation for verses 8–11?

What glorifies God according to verse 8?

What is a disciple? Look up the word and write your own definition.

How is a disciple to abide in Christ's love according to verse 10?

How is this connected with bearing fruit?

Look at verse 11. What is the result of abiding in Christ's love through obedience?

DIGEST THE BIG IDEAS

What kind of relationship does Jesus encourage his disciples to have with his words?

Why is obedience a fruit of abiding in Christ and his words abiding in you?

Read John 14:23. What is the result of loving Jesus? What kind of relationship with God is the result?

Read 1 John 2:3–6. What evidence demonstrates that a believer is in Christ?

What is Jesus talking about in John 15:8–11?

What is he saying about it?

What is the main idea of this passage?

What did you learn about God, Jesus Christ, or the gospel from today's study?

GROW IN GODLINESS

How might the main idea of John 15:8–11 apply to your circumstances?

Circle the way you will respond to God's Word today.

Today I will...   believe   act   repent   worship   pray

Use this space for your response or to plan how you will respond throughout your day.

Write the verse, attribute of God, or gospel truth you will meditate on today.

Day Four | Fellowship in the Word

Bees know better than to try to do life on their own. In the cold weather of winter, bees huddle together around the queen bee, vibrating their bodies to create extra warmth. As the bees on the outer edges of the huddle get cold, they rotate to the inner circle, each bee taking a turn sacrificing their own heat on the outer edge to keep the entire colony warm and the queen protected.

In the summer, bees still focus on what's best for the colony. When they find a particularly good source of nectar, they don't keep it to themselves. They communicate its location through a kind of dance to the other bees in the hive. They pass along the bounty, ensuring that the colony will thrive through its interdependent relationships.

God also created humans to be better together. We aren't only dependent on God but also on fellowship with his people. I (Maggie) recently faced one of the most challenging seasons of my adult life. I struggled to open God's Word. I despaired over the loss of a future I had mistakenly assumed was certain. I worried about whether or not my family would have enough.

When I couldn't hold it together, my church family held me up. They graciously gave of their resources in clear acts of God's provision for our family. They checked on us constantly. They sent us gentle reminders of God's truth. Eventually, it was the help of friends from church that alleviated the difficult circumstances my family was faced with. When we were in crisis, they gladly moved to the edges of the little huddle of our church body and gave up their own warmth to care for ours. And they did it all joyfully. When I was tempted to feel like God was taking from me, they were living proof that God gives all I need.

Christians aren't meant to do life on their own. God made us to support each other—through serving, teaching, helping, and reminding each other of the honey of God's Word. In today's study of John 15, you'll see that when we abide in Jesus, who laid down his life for us, we respond by laying down our lives out of love for others (John 15:13). We are friends of Jesus if we obey his teaching (John 15:14), and as our friend, Jesus tells us what he hears from the Father (John 15:15). So if we are to imitate Christ in our friendships, we not only lay down our lives for our friends, we also share with them the truth of God's Word.

Throughout history, honey has been considered to have all kinds of medicinal uses. Today, we know that honey can help heal burns more quickly, is a natural antibiotic, and may even help alleviate the side effects of cancer treatment. The honey of God's Word is like a balm to the wounded soul. When we not only serve the family of God but open God's Word together through preaching and teaching or just one-on-one relationships, God's Word brings healing. Of course, we must grow in our discernment of how and when to use God's Word wisely to help a friend, but we shouldn't neglect doing so because we're afraid we may misuse it.

If you don't feel comfortable talking about God's Word with your friends, you're probably in the majority of Christian women. Why is it so hard? Because we never practice. Practice builds habits. You might find it easiest to start by attending a formal Bible study with a small group of women. Maybe you're in one, going through this material right now, or maybe God is calling you to invite a group of women to do this study together now that you're about to finish it. When you get practice talking through the questions at a weekly Bible study, humbly admitting when you're not sure about your answer, or joyously sharing about how God used his Word to intersect your life in a specific way that week, you tear down the walls of awkwardness that often surround sharing about God's Word. As you talk consistently about God's Word with one group of women, you'll find that it's easier to bring it up in your relationships with others.

Over time, you may find it difficult not to talk about God's Word. After all, the more time you spend in it, the sweeter it becomes to you, and you'll begin to feel compelled to share that sweetness with others. And if right now you're thinking about a specific friend or group of friends that you'd like to talk about God's Word with, brave the awkwardness and be the one to go first. Going first opens the door for other women to follow you into deeper intimacy with God through his Word and deeper intimacy with each other.

 Pray for humility and insight before you study God's Word.

GATHER KNOWLEDGE

Read John 15:12–17. There are a lot of repeated words in this short passage. Make a list of as many as you notice and include the number of times each word appears.

Even though the sentences are short and clear, the passage as a whole can actually feel a little confusing because of the repetition. Next to each verse reference, rewrite the verse in your own words to bring clarity to what Jesus is saying.

John 15:12

John 15:13

John 15:14

John 15:15

John 15:16

John 15:17

Put a dot next to any verse that includes a command. Then put a star next to the verse that you think is most important or summarizes the passage the best.

DIGEST THE BIG IDEAS

Read John 17:26. Jesus is praying to God the Father. What is the purpose of Jesus making the Father known?

Read Colossians 3:16. What actions of fellowship are the result of the Word of Christ dwelling richly within us?

What is Jesus talking about in John 15:12–17?

What is he saying about it?

What is the main idea of this passage?

What did you learn about God, Jesus Christ, or the gospel from today's study?

GROW IN GODLINESS

How might the main idea of John 15:12–17 apply to your circumstances?

Circle the way you will respond to God's Word today.

Today I will...   believe   act   repent   worship   pray

Use this space for your response or to plan how you will respond throughout your day.

Write the verse, attribute of God, or gospel truth you will meditate on today.

Day Five | The Fruit of the Word

What's so great about honey anyway? Why has it been highly valued for thousands of years? Why am I (Maggie) willing to make a special trip to the farmers market just to get the good, local stuff? It's simple, really—honey delights our senses. The plodding pour of golden, glassy honey soothes the soul. Its stickiness is lip-smacking on a warm slice of bread (but we won't talk about it on a toddler's grubby fingers). And the smell! I wouldn't be surprised if heaven smells like honey. But most of all, honey tastes sweet and rich and downright yummy. Honey is simply a delight.

Remember the beekeeping experience I (Gretchen) mentioned at the very beginning of this study? After seeing firsthand how honey bees make honey, my husband and I were so excited to buy a little jar of honey as a memento. Our excitement plummeted when we went to pay and realized it was $34 for a laughably tiny jar. Tight-grinned, we paid the exorbitant rate to have something to remember our experience by (and maybe to avoid the awkwardness of putting it back). Whether you get your honey at a tourist experience, the farmers market, or Costco, honey is costly. Doing Bible study is costly too. It'll sometimes cost you sleep or time on your phone or a lazy Saturday afternoon, but it's always worth it. If you consistently and diligently dig into God's Word, you'll reap a harvest of fruit by being in the presence of your Savior.

So keep your eyes on Jesus as you search the pages of God's Word. As you focus on your Savior, beholding his power and glory, you will become more like him. Joy in Jesus empowers you to bear fruit. May you embrace all that you have in Christ and live from his abundance, remembering this: God's presence is a promise, and fullness of joy is your eternal hope. So when you close this study, commit to continuing to open God's Word. Pay the cost of diligently gathering knowledge, digesting big ideas, and growing in godliness, and you will soon grow to enjoy the sweetness of knowing God through his Word and declare with the psalmist:

> How sweet are your words to my taste,
> sweeter than honey to my mouth!
>
> PSALM 119:103

Pray for humility and insight before you study God's Word.

GATHER KNOWLEDGE

Read John 15:1–17. Note how many times these words are used in this passage.

Abide(s)

Fruit

Love(d)

Look at verse 11. What do you think the phrase *these things* refers to?

Why has Jesus spoken these things to his disciples?

DIGEST THE BIG IDEAS

What connection does this passage make between abiding, fruit, and love?

What connection does joy have to this relationship between abiding, fruit, and love?

Read Hebrews 12:2. What did Jesus endure? What was set before Jesus as his goal? Where does Jesus remain now?

Read Philippians 4:4. What command is given twice? What is the focus and source of a believer's joy?

What did you learn about God, Jesus Christ, or the gospel from today's study?

GROW IN GODLINESS

Circle the way you will respond to God's Word today.

Today I will...   believe   act   repent   worship   pray

Use this space for your response or to plan how you will respond throughout your day.

Write the verse, attribute of God, or gospel truth you will meditate on today.

Session Six Viewer Guide

_____
_____
_____
_____
_____
_____
_____
_____
_____
_____
_____
_____
_____
_____
_____
_____
_____
_____
_____
_____

QUESTIONS FOR DISCUSSION OR REFLECTION

What's one spiritual discipline you will attach to a daily habit this week? Which habit will you attach it to?

What new skills for studying God's Word have you developed through this Bible study?

How will you continue the discipline of studying God's Word now that you've completed this Bible study?

What have you learned in this Bible study that has grown your love for God and his Word?

Build Your Bible Study Library

We recommend that every woman utilizes a comprehensive study Bible and these free resources as she studies God's Word:

- Book summary videos on bibleproject.com
- Commentaries on thegospelcoalition.org
- Introductions to the Bible on blueletterbible.org under the Study tab

If you want to create a library of resources to help you dig deeper in God's Word, here are our recommendations.

Study Bibles

ESV Study Bible

CSB Spurgeon Study Bible

ESV Literary Study Bible

Reference Books

Mounce's Complete Expository Dictionary of Old and New Testament Words

Strong's Exhaustive Concordance of the Bible

A Visual Theology Guide to the Bible by Tim Challies and Josh Byers

Commentaries

ESV Expository Commentary Series by Crossway

God's Word For You Series by The Good Book Company

Books about Bible Study

Biblical Theology by Nick Roark and Robert Cline

Christ from Beginning to End by Trent Hunter and Stephen Wellum

How to Read the Bible for All Its Worth by Gordon D. Fee and Douglas Stuart

How to Read the Bible in Changing Times by Mark L. Strauss

Jesus on Every Page by David Murray

Main Idea Examples

WEEK ONE | STUDY THE WORD

Day Two | Gather

If we are to love God with all of ourselves, we must be constantly teaching, discussing, and remembering God's commands in our everyday lives.

Day Three | Digest

We experience the blessing of relationship with God when we delight in and meditate on God's Word.

Day Four | Grow

God reveals himself in both creation and his Word, and through his Word he instructs us on how to live lives that are pleasing and acceptable acts of worship before him.

Day Five | Enjoy

When we study God's Word and delight in it, we experience abundant life through knowing and loving God.

WEEK THREE | THE GOOD NEWS OF THE WORD

Day One | Creation

Our all-powerful God created the universe and called it good, created humans in his own image, and gave humans the roles of cultivators and caretakers.

Day Two | Fall

Because of Adam and Eve's disobedience, creation is cursed and all people sin and fall short of God's glory and desperately need the hope of a Savior.

Day Three | Redemption

Jesus died on the cross and rose again so that those who have faith in him could be redeemed, fulfilling the prophecies and promises of the Old Testament.

Day Four | Consummation

Both present and past believers place their hope in the final consummation of God's promises, when God will create a new heaven and new earth to dwell with his people forever.

References

WEEK ONE | STUDY THE WORD

1. "World's Oldest Honey," *Bee Mission* (blog), September 12, 2019, https://beemission.com/blogs/news/worlds-oldest-honey.

2. Joe Hanson, "How Do Bees Make Honey?" YouTube video, March 28, 2019, https://www.youtube.com/watch?v=nZlEjDLJCmg.

3. Gordon D. Fee and Douglas Stuart, *How to Read the Bible for All Its Worth* (Grand Rapids, MI: Zondervan Academic, 2014), 18.

4. Fee and Stuart, *How to Read the Bible for All Its Worth*, 30.

5. Mark L. Strauss, *How to Read the Bible in Changing Times* (Grand Rapids, MI: Baker Books, 2011), 78.

6. Strauss, *How to Read the Bible in Changing Times*, 102.

WEEK TWO | THE UNCHANGING WORD

7. Fee and Stuart, *How to Read the Bible for All Its Worth*, 22.

8. Tim Challies and Josh Byers, *A Visual Theology Guide to the Bible* (Grand Rapids, MI: Zondervan, 2019), 28.

9. Dictionary.com, s.v. "Genre," accessed January 19, 2024, https://www.dictionary.com/browse/genre.

10. Kristie Anyabwile, *Literarily: How Understanding Bible Genres Transforms Bible Study* (Chicago, IL: Moody Publishers, 2022), 53.

11. Strauss, *How to Read the Bible in Changing Times*, 146.

12. Strauss, *How to Read the Bible in Changing Times*, 178.

13. Anyabwile, *Literarily*, 136.

14. Strauss, *How to Read the Bible in Changing Times*, 194.

WEEK THREE | THE GOOD NEWS OF THE WORD

15. Kanoe Riedel, "Festooning: Three Theories About the Mysterious Bee-havior Stumping Scientists and Beekeepers Alike," Beepods, September 3, 2020, https://www.beepods.com/festooning-three-theories-about-the-mysterious-bee-havior-stumping-scientists-and-beekeepers-alike/.

16. Grateful for the wisdom and work of Lauren Weir in defining and clarifying the descriptions of the four parts of the redemption story that we use throughout this week of study.

17. "Christian History: Fanny Crosby," Christianity Today, accessed February 2, 2024, https://www.christianitytoday.com/history/people/poets/fanny-crosby.html.

18. Fanny Crosby, "Take the World, but Give Me Jesus," 1879, accessed February 2, 2024, https://hymnary.org/text/take_the_world_but_give_me_jesus_all_its.

WEEK FOUR | TRANSFORMED BY THE WORD

19. Julia Higgins, *Empowered and Equipped: Bible Exposition for Women Who Teach the Scriptures* (Nashville, TN: B&H Academic, 2022), 119.
20. Higgins, *Empowered and Equipped*, 119.
21. C.S. Lewis, "First and Second Things," in *God in the Dock: Essays on Theology and Ethics* (Grand Rapids, MI: Eerdmans, 1994 revised edition), 280.

WEEK FIVE | THE WORD IN EVERY SEASON

22. David Golinkin, "Torah is as sweet as honey," The Jerusalem Post, May 22, 2007, https://www.jpost.com/Jewish-World/Judaism/Torah-is-as-sweet-as-honey.
23. This concept is adapted from the 3–5 Method that we first learned from Abbey Wedgeworth. Read more about this method here: https://openthebible.org/article/studying-gods-word-when-youre-tired-and-busy/.

WEEK SIX | THE WORD IN EVERYDAY LIFE

24. Timothy Keller, *Prayer: Experiencing Awe and Intimacy with God* (New York, NY: Penguin Group, 2014), 148.
25. John Piper, *Reading the Bible Supernaturally* (Wheaton, IL: Crossway Books, 2017), 254–255, 269–273.
26. Jen Wilkin, *Women of the Word: How to Study the Bible with Both Our Hearts and Our Minds* (Wheaton, IL: Crossway Books, 2014), 31.